RÉMY DESQUESNES

NORMANDY 1944

Éditions **OUEST-FRANCE**

PREPARATIONS AND D-DAY
JUNE 6, 1944

Opposite: Landing barge heading towards Omaha Beach on June 6, 1944.

Overlord:
a war machine devised by the British

Once the North Africa campaign had been successfully completed, the US authorities were reluctant to pursue operations in the Mediterranean, putting pressure on the United Kingdom to open a front on the Channel in the fall of 1943. Washington considered this to be the only strategy that would bring down the *Reich*. In early 1943, in order to prepare for this future landing on the banks of western Europe – undoubtedly the most complex operation of the entire Second World War – the Americans called for the creation of a military staff tasked with drawing up the plans. They cleverly entrusted the command of this 'brain-trust' to a British General. Known as 'COSSAC' (from 'Chief of Staff to Supreme Allied Commander'), this staff, based in London and dominated by British strategists, would choose the sector for the future assault, develop Operation Fortitude, which was designed to deceive the enemy over the Allies' intentions, gather information about the *Wehrmacht* using 'Ultra', and devise new secret weapons. As well as the range of special tanks designed to overcome the defenses of the Atlantic Wall, these weapons included the 'mulberry' or artificial harbor, an unprecedented innovation; 'gooseberries', breakwaters positioned in front of each of the assault beaches; and 'Pluto', an undersea oil pipeline, another British brainwave. It might also be said that it was Montgomery's strategic thinking that prevailed in the amphibious assault on the Normandy beaches and in the ensuing lengthy battle. While the Red Army was fighting to the death against the *Wehrmacht* and the Americans were producing hundreds of thousands of tanks, airplanes, guns and assault craft, the British, with their Prime Minister and their Generals, were devising, planning and conducting the conflict.

Among the numerous military actions carried out during the Second World War on the various theaters of operations, the Battle of Normandy (6 June-21 August 1944) should be considered one of the most decisive operations, after El Alamein, Stalingrad, Tunis (May 1943) and Kursk (summer 1943). Even though it did not put an end to the war and it took place late in the proceedings, the Allied victory in the Falaise pocket was a decisive step on the way to final victory.

The Normandy operation was not the only landing carried out by the Allies during the last World War. The Channel operation, which underwent a series of adjustments – its original code name, 'Roundup', was changed at the Quebec conference to 'Overlord' – drew from the lessons of previous more or less unsuccessful amphibious attempts. Before Normandy, not mentioning the operations led by Admiral King in the far Pacific, there was the costly disaster in Dieppe in August 1942, a clumsy assault on the coasts of north Africa in November 1942, a full-scale replica in July 1943 on the southern coast of Sicily, and two other training exercises on the shores of the Italian peninsula, in Salerno and Anzio. One might say that, before performing their sonata to perfection in the Channel, the Allies spent several long years practicing their scales!

It is worthwhile spending a few moments considering these combined operations that took place prior to Normandy, since no historical or military event can ever be fully understood without first going back to its origins.

A Poster from 1944.

Picking up shipwrecked survivors as the forces are re-embarked after the failure of the raid on Dieppe.

INVASIONS BEFORE NORMANDY

"The United States was just getting into its stride in the mobilization and training of its armies, navies and air forces. [...] The great bulk of the fighting equipment, naval, air, and ground, needed for the invasion did not exist. [...] In the summer of 1942 it took a very considerable faith, not to say optimism, to look forward to the day when the potentialities of the United States would be fully developed. [...] This attitude of faith was demanded at all superior headquarters. Any expression of defeatism or any failure to push ahead in confidence was instant cause for relief from duty, and all officers knew it."

D. D. Eisenhower

Dieppe

Operation Jubilee

August 19, 1942

Of all the amphibious operations carried out by the Allies on the western front, Dieppe stands apart. Occurring roughly midway between the retreat from Dunkirk and the Normandy invasion, Jubilee was the first large-scale attempt at direct aggression against the *Wehrmacht* along the shores of France. An operation resting almost exclusively on the shoulders of the Canadian army, impatient to get into combat, Dieppe was a failure that would be exploited by Nazi propaganda to demonstrate that it was impossible for an assailant to breach the barrier that was the Atlantic Wall.

Canadians in training.

The assault fleet on the way to Dieppe.

Fockewulff 190: German fighter, here on the Théville airfield (Maupertus) near Cherbourg. During the day of August 19, the *Luftwaffe* would lose almost fifty aircraft (medium-sized fighters and bombers).

Map of Operation Jubilee produced by the Germans on the basis of captured Allied documents and published in the October 1942 edition of the magazine *Signal*.

It should be stressed from the outset that, like the daring attack launched by British commandos against the German radar station at Bruneval or against the big dry dock at the port of Saint-Nazaire, in February-March 1942, what German propaganda would refer to as the *Landung bei Dieppe* (the Dieppe invasion) was really no more than a large-scale raid. The actual mission, in August 1942, of the 6,000 men, 5,000 of whom belonged to General McNaughton's 1st Canadian Army, was to come ashore along a front about twelve miles wide either side of the seaside resort of Dieppe, to stay on land for the duration

Jubilee was the most deadly operation led by the Canadian army.

British bomber above the city of Dieppe (the harbor can be seen at the top left). During that one day, the RAF would lose almost 120 aircraft as a result of the enemy fighters, the *Flak*, collisions and firing errors. For the British air force, Dieppe would remain the most costly day of the entire war.

of two tides, that is about twelve hours, and to inflict maximum damage on the enemy (coastal defenses, the airfield at Saint-Aubin, a radar station, port installations, railways, fuel depots...). Once those objectives had been achieved, the assailants were to withdraw and return to England. As we see, there was no question of a proper landing operation aimed at creating a permanent beachhead along the Channel coast from which to launch subsequent operations against the occupying forces.

Whilst the assault fleet comprising 250 warships and landing craft was approaching the French coast, in the small hours of August 19, 1942, a few Allied units met a German convoy coming down the Channel. A violent confrontation ensued which alerted the defenders on land. All that they had to do then was to prepare a welcoming party for the commando that was about to set foot on land on the beach at Le Puys. Fighting an unequal and hopeless battle, the gallant Canadian detachment was literally mown down by machine-guns hidden in prearranged combat positions. At the other end of the assault area, apart from destroying the shore battery at Varengeville, the attackers, deprived of the support of the tanks stuck on the pebble beach at Dieppe,

52

L'

9, rue LOUIS-LE-GRAND (2

Adresse Télégraphique Œuvre

Chèque postal n° 1046

UN IMPORTANT
débarquement britannique
PRÈS DE DIEPPE
a subi un échec total

Une première vague transbordée au large sur 3 à 400 canots a atteint la côte à 6 h. 5 protégée par 13 à 15 croiseurs et contre-torpilleurs et par l'aviation de chasse.

Elle a été rejetée à la mer

Un « Spitfire » abattu au-dessus de la Manche est venu s'écraser dans les dunes. (Photo SAFARA, exclusivité Œuvre).

La deuxième ligne était composée de 32 transports et 3 cargos. Elle n'a pu intervenir et a subi des pertes considérables sous les bombardements de l'artillerie côtière et des attaques de la Luftwaffe

A 16 heures, il n'y avait plus un seul soldat ennemi sur le continent

LE BILAN DE LA VICTORIEUSE RIPOSTE ALLEMANDE :

28 chars d'assaut anéantis ; 3 contre-torpilleurs, 2 torpilleurs, 4 transports, 1 vedette rapide coulés ; 5 croiseurs ou grands contre-torpilleurs et 2 transports endommagés ; 83 avions abattus ; plus de 1500 prisonniers, dont 60 officiers canadiens et des pertes en hommes extrêmement élevées

The front page of the Monday August 31 edition of *L'Œuvre*, a newspaper entirely in the pay of the enemy.

had to turn back in the face of the vigorous German response. In the center of the sector of operations, the attack on the beach of Dieppe resulted in almost total failure. The Canadian infantry soldiers were pinned down under murderous enemy fire. In a word, Jubilee was an unmitigated disaster, and, except at Berneval and Varengeville, not a single objective had been reached. By evening on August 19, losses were catastrophic: on returning to the quays at Newhaven, more than one man in two was missing and the number of killed alone reached nearly a thousand. Given such carnage for an operation that had hardly lasted nine hours, what then would it be like on the day the Allies made their big return to the continent? After this brutal experience, the Canadian survivors who, a few days earlier, had been keen to take on the Germans, were now convinced that war is in no way a game and that any battle is a cruel and merciless business.

It is true that Jubilee remains the bloodiest expedition that the Canadian army had ever embarked upon and the greatest military disaster in the history of that country. However, the Allied command would draw some useful lessons from this costly adventure for future operations, such as the need to carry out an aerial bombing prior to any assault against a fortified coastline and to ensure permanent air cover for the beachhead. Dieppe also showed that it was essential to ship across artillery to provide support for the troops on the ground, to maintain the element of surprise right up to the last moment, to use paratroops as a diversionary force before launching the seaborne assault and to provide better training for the men. However, this was not the main lesson to be learnt. Although in an inhuman way, without any doubt, Dieppe would provide an answer to the crucial question that the Allied strategists were asking themselves: what were the chances of success of an invasion against a port defended and fortified by the Germans? In showing that any frontal assault against a continental port was heading for certain failure, Jubilee would encourage the Allied chiefs of staff to pursue research towards perfecting a revolutionary combined operation enabling a large-scale landing to take place away from the conventional installations of a large port. 'Mulberries' (the code name for the artificial harbors), a technological challenge and genuine secret weapon for the Allies, were designed to aid the Allies' return to the continent. It is clear, therefore, that Overlord was based on the lessons learnt from Jubilee.

It was on the coasts of north Africa, as Churchill had wished, and not on the shores of the Channel, that the first big Anglo-American landing took place, three months after Dieppe. Code-named Torch (the torch of freedom), and placed under the command of the American General Eisenhower, the operation was the first stage in the British battle plan designed to attack the Axis powers in their more distant conquests.

Lieutenant-Colonel Lord Lovat back in Newhaven after having destroyed the Varengeville battery with his commando. He would be seen in Bénouville on June 6 accompanied by his piper.

North Africa

Operation Torch

November 8, 1942

Wresting the initiative from the Axis in a secondary theater of operations, chasing the Italians and Germans out of Africa and keeping the promise made to Stalin in 1942 to open a second front, these were the strategic objectives of Torch. The sector chosen for the attack was nearly 950 miles long, stretching from Casablanca to Algiers, that is to say along both the Atlantic and the Mediterranean coasts. Such an over-extended

With his 8th Army, Montgomery would finally teach Rommel a lesson in El Alamein in November 1942.

Opposite, left: The most popular general of the *Wehrmacht,* Rommel suffered from the fact that priority was given to the Russian front during the winter of 1942-1943. Hitler's mistrust of the *Afrika Korps* soon gave Rommel food for thought.

assault front can be explained quite simply by the Allies' refusal to run the risk of finding themselves trapped in the Mediterranean by a possible blockade of the Straits of Gibraltar. Three landings were planned: an exclusively American contingent in the Casablanca area, on Morocco's Atlantic seaboard, and the two others carried out by mixed Anglo-American forces in the region of Oran and Algiers. Once a beachhead had been successfully established, the Allied troops were to march

The American assault fleet approaching Morocco's Atlantic coast.

Fedhala. Patton would land on this shore.

eastwards and join up with Montgomery's army coming from the western border of Egypt, thus gripping the Axis forces in a huge vice.

Comprising three Task Forces (autonomous naval forces), the Allied armada comprised an assault force (more than 200 warships, including several aircraft-carriers), a protection

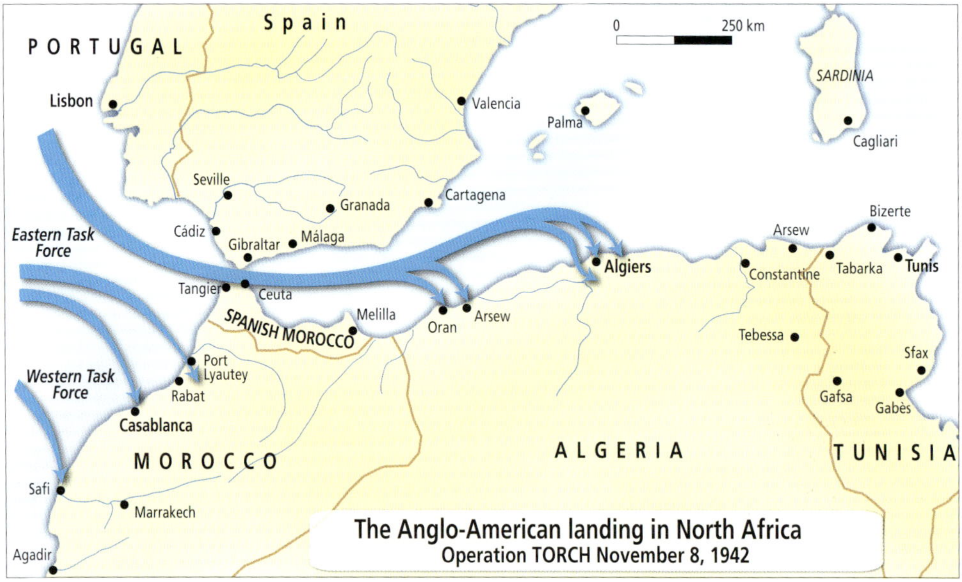

Australian soldiers in the jebels of North Africa.

EXTRACT FROM A LEAFLET DISTRIBUTED IN NORTH AFRICA ON THE DAY OF THE INVASION (NOVEMBER 8, 1942)

"We are coming to liberate you. [...] We are only coming to destroy your enemies; we don't want to harm you [...] and we will leave as soon as the threat represented by Germany and Italy has been dispelled."

D. D. Eisenhower

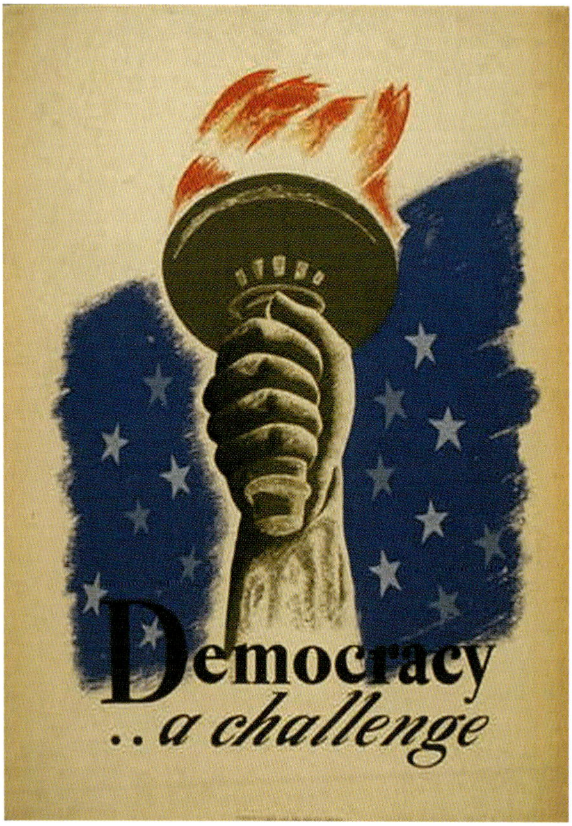

The torch of democracy and liberty, two ideals shared by the western Allies.

force for the convoys, a force carrying supplies and a little more than a hundred troop transport ships and landing craft. Setting off from Portland and Norfolk, Virginia, in this month of October 1942, the Western Task Force exclusively comprising units belonging to the US Navy followed the same course as Christopher Columbus in the opposite direction with the *Niña* and the *Pinta*, 450 years before. Heading towards Oran and Algiers, the two other convoys had departed from English ports. In principle, the plan was to disembark 35,000 soldiers onto the Moroccon coast, and just as many on the Algerian coastline, during the night and day of November 8th. With the coast having limited fortification, it had been decided that the landing operation would not be preceded by any aerial or naval bombardments of the beach's defenses. Even though the situation was dragging on, the disembarkation proceeded more or less as planned, so once the sporadic French resistance had been overcome, it can be said that on November 10, the Anglo-American had control of the entire north-west coast of the African continent, from southern Morocco to the heights of Algiers. Overall, losses in men had been slight, and only about thirty warships, mostly smaller units, had been sunk by torpedoes fired from enemy submarines.

As for the Allied commanders, they were under no illusions and perfectly aware that the easy success of Torch was due to a set of favorable conditions: the absence of coastal fortifications, total surprise and a poor response from the defenders. Some remembered that the Canadian attackers had received a very different welcome three months before in the Channel. In spite of its success, Torch, which had progressed infinitely slower than expected, still looked like a match that had been fought without training.

On the evening of November 8, for example, in the American sector, only half of the troops had been landed and, due to the violence of the ebb tide, there had been considerable holdups in the unloading of equipment and, consequently, a severe backlog in the units' departure times. To this waste of time, partly due to the inadequate training of the soldiers in the use of large scramble nets hanging down the side of the transport ships into the assault barges, must be added the loss of equipment. Collisions, maneuvering errors, landing craft coming ashore with the bow door facing out to sea, lowering the ramps of the assault barges too soon, obliging the soldiers to swim under

Contrasting methods: an American four-engined plane, the flagship of American technology, flying over yoked animals led by a *fellah* (Morocco, early 1943).

enemy fire (fortunately not too aggressive here) or flooding the vehicle or tracked engine motors, are attributable to incompetence on the part of the crews. To offset the slowness of the comings and goings between the shore and the ships anchored offshore, the marines

GIBRALTAR

"In November 1942, the Allied nations possessed, except for the Gibraltar Fortress, not a single spot of ground in all the region of western Europe, and in the Mediterranean area, nothing west of Malta. Britain's Gibraltar made possible the invasion of northwest Africa. Without it the vital air cover would not have been quickly established on the North African fields."

D. D. Eisenhower

tended to overload the landing craft, which sank in the slightest gust of wind in the open sea or in the heavy breakers along the coast. Thus, in some cases, losses of landing craft type vessels exceeded 90 per cent of the numbers engaged! Similarly, owing to a lack of documents (panoramic aerial photographs with information about the coasts as seen from out to sea, three-dimensional sketches...) and because of the darkness and coastal currents along the African shore, the pilots had great difficulty in locating their landing beaches. The result was a dispersal of the forces, the confusion of the different units involved and chaotic unloading (vehicles on one beach with their drivers on another). A further embarrassment was the lack of special LST type ships (Landing Ship Tank) capable of transporting and unloading armored vehicles along the beaches at the same time as the assault infantry. During Torch, the large majority of the tanks were transported on board conventional ships whose unloading required the prior capture of port facilities; hence, once again, more or less lengthy delays, idle waiting, and lost time. Essential to ensure the success of any amphibious operation, the LSTs, big tank transport ships capable of running aground directly onto the beaches, initially designed by the Americans for their operations in the Pacific, would make their appearance for the first time in the theater of European operations, in Sicily, in July 1943.

Having chased the Axis out of Africa in May 1943, the objective of the Allies was now to get a foothold on the continent of Europe through Sicily, to restore free navigation in the Mediterranean, to eliminate a defeated Italy from the war with Germany and to make her change sides. Thanks to Husky (the code name of the Sicily landing), the Anglo-Americans were hoping both to relieve the Russian front, by drawing and holding about twenty German divisions in Italy, and to make things easier for the big cross-Channel invasion planned for May 1st, 1944.

Above:

Following the invasion of the free zone by Germany in retaliation against the Allied landing in Africa, Darlan, head of the Marines, ordered the French fleet anchored in Toulon to scuttle its ships. Almost 80 boats of all sorts (cruisers, battleships, torpedo boats, submarines…) were set alight and sunk, without great danger for the admirals. We can easily imagine the disappointment of the Allies at seeing this magnificent fighting instrument go up in smoke.

Opposite:

Stalingrad (February 1943): the resounding Soviet victory came just a few months before the Allied victory in Tunis in May 1943, where some 400,000 Italo-German soldiers would be taken prisoner. Referring to the Axis defeat in Tunisia as "Tunisgrad", Allied propaganda tried to emphasize the similarities with the Russian victory on the banks of the Volga. After these two surrenders, the strategic initiative passed into the hands of the Allied coalition.

Sicily

Operation Husky

July 10, 1943

Initially, the Allied commanders had planned to carry out a double landing, one on the north coast and the other on the south coast, in order to take the Italians and Germans in a pincer movement. As this project went contrary to the sacred principle of concentration of the forces, it was finally abandoned in favor of a single landing in the south-east corner of the island, between the ports of Licata to the west and Syracuse to the east, along a 100 mile front. All this southern corner of the island had the advantage

The Allied leaders: Monty, Bradley and Patton.

Opposite: Marauder bombers on their way back from the mission off the Sicilian coast.

of being within range of permanent cover from Allied fighter planes based in Malta and the airfields of Tunisia. However, although it had big sandy or pebbly beaches, this sector was less suitable for beaching the big landing craft (LST and LCT - Landing Craft Tank)

The Landing Ship Tank (LST), a craft capable of running aground next to the shore, and DUKWs, amphibious trucks, were two innovations introduced during the operation in Sicily.

because of the unfavorable gradient of the shore and the fact that, unlike in the Pacific, there were no coral reefs off these beaches but instead shallow waters running parallel to the shore. British troops under Montgomery were to land in the eastern sector, on a 40 mile front between Catania and Messina, and Bradley's Americans to the west, on a front of similar length between Gela and Licata. Between the two assault forces, again placed under the command of General Eisenhower, there stretched a corridor about fifteen miles wide. A year later, a comparable disposition of forces was used in Normandy, but on a front only half that length, due to the more systematic defenses. After their defeat in Tunisia in May 1943, the Germans were expecting an operation in the Mediterranean – "something was in the wind...", wrote US Navy Admiral Samuel Morison – so the Allies set up a deception plan intended to make the Intelligence Services of Admiral Canaris believe that the

next expedition would take place in Sardinia or the Peloponnesus. To confirm Hitler's fears, the Allied air forces began a program of bombing attacks against airfields, roads, bridges, tunnels and railways, particularly in Sardinia.

For the operation in Sicily, the Allies had gathered together sufficient means to launch a gigantic assault. Never before had an armada been assembled numbering over 3,500 ships of all kinds including 750 warships, or an air fleet of 4,000 British and American units with orders to disable the enemy air power, carry out various transport operations and ensure permanent air cover for the beachhead. Prior to the dropping of two airborne divisions whose mission was to destroy or capture a certain number of nerve centers, the seaborne invasion took place by moonlight, starting at 3 a.m. on July 10. It involved the landing of 8 infantry divisions (IDs), 24,000 vehicles, 1,800 guns and 600 tanks! With a first wave of more than 160,000 men, the initial assault in Sicily set a record that was never equaled, even in Normandy a year later. *"Husky is the largest amphibious operation of the war, at least on the first day."* This statement would later be qualified by *"on the European front"*. The Allied assault on Okinawa, in the Pacific, on April 1, 1945, remains the greatest concentration of amphibious forces of all time, and probably the last ever, with the dawning of the new age of atomic weapons.

The opening bow door of the LSTs meant that they could land the armored vehicles which were vital for a break-out.

From July 11, D+1, the Americans (and not for the last time, we are tempted to write, now that after Omaha we know the rest of the story) were to face a vigorous counter-attack led by German armored vehicles rushing down the slopes of the hills above the narrow Sicilian beaches. The enemy's plan paid off: a vicious offensive was launched at the critical moment that follows any amphibious operation when the beachhead lacks depth,

Canadian troops in Sicily.

and before the attacker can muster his entire fighting force. Here, the Americans were all the more vulnerable due to the considerable backlog in unloading operations that had built up because of heavy seas and the presence of sandbanks, which meant that the large LSTs had to beach much earlier than intended, so far out as to make unloading impossible without first setting up a roadway on metal pontoons.

Finally, after many hours of fierce combat, massive intervention of the seaborne artillery and the fighter bombers saved the day. In spite of their prompt and vigorous reaction, the Germans were unable to throw the Americans back into the sea. For the German command, after July 1943 the lesson was clear: without air cover from the *Luftwaffe*, any counter-attack launched by the *Panzers* was doomed to failure. Once the crisis was over, it remained for the Allies to join up the two assault sectors in a single continuous beachhead enabling wider maneuvers to be attempted, with the capture of enemy airfields and the construction of air-strips a top priority in order to maintain control in the air and subsequently capture a few large ports (Syracuse, Palermo...).

With the benefit of the lessons learnt during Torch and the experience gained by the Americans in the Pacific against the Japanese, Husky was a big step forward in the history of amphibious operations. Only a year had passed since the disaster at Dieppe and eight months since the Torch adventure. Indeed it is true to say that Sicily prefigures Normandy more than it is reminiscent of Africa. In both cases, in the Mediterranean and in the Channel, a powerful assault was carried out on open beaches, away from the installations of a large continental port, thanks to an armada of specialized ships (LST, LSI – Landing Ship Infantry, LCT) capable of running directly aground. However, as in June 1944, the Allies were to employ two artificial harbors, it would be more correct to state that Overlord was a variation rather than a repetition of the Sicilian experiment. Having said that, if we consider the general organization, the articulation of the various forces engaged, the progress of the operation, the diversionary maneuvers, the use of air photography, radar, submarines used as marker buoys, amphibious trucks, the commandos and gliders used to transport airborne troops including the 82nd US Airborne Division that would later drop over Sainte-Mère-Eglise, and the names of the commanders (Eisenhower, Montgomery, Bradley, Patton, Ramsay, Hewitt, Tedder...), the obvious conclusion is to draw a parallel between Husky and Overlord.

By mid-August 1943, after five weeks of violent combat involving almost half a million Allied soldiers, Mussolini was toppled and the island was freed. Using Sicily as a springboard, the Allies decided to push on into southern Italy: whilst the British and Canadians were to cross the Straits of Messina, on September 3rd, and land in the Gulf of Taranto, the US 5th Army of General Clark would land to the rear of the German defenders further north, in the Naples area, in the Gulf of Salerno.

By forcing Hitler to send considerable reinforcements to Italy just as the Germans were carrying out their third summer offensive in the USSR, Husky contributed to the Soviets' victory in Kursk.

Salerno

Operation Avalanche

September 9, 1943

Executed against their wishes by the Americans, the landing at Salerno (Operation Avalanche) was on altogether a smaller scale than Husky. The same was true of the next operation, at Anzio, in January 1944. In a hurry to get the war over, after Sicily the American chiefs-of-staff had only one objective: to prepare the Allies' big return to the continent of Europe thanks to an assault to be launched from across the Channel in the spring of 1944. For General Marshall, chief-of-staff of the US Army, it was only from the beachhead secured in the Bay of the Seine that the Allies could hope to see off the *Reich*, and not by dispersing their forces in several theaters of war. Faithful to this strategic approach, the Americans agreed not to take part in the operations in Italy on the condition that the British would not contest the launch of the major Channel offensive planned for early May 1944.

In choosing to land at Salerno, the Allies' objective was to facilitate progress northwards up the peninsula for Montgomery's troops and capture the port of Naples which was crucial to get supplies to troops whose mission was to deliver Rome. From a strategic viewpoint, the possession of airfields in Italy (in the Foggia plain) would make it possible to bomb German cities from the

Canadian tank in the Italian countryside.

Landing Ship Infantry (LSI), a craft specialized in transporting troops.

south and also oilfields exploited by the Axis in Romania.

Launched in late summer 1943, Operation Avalanche took place in one of the most beautiful bays in the Mediterranean not far from Vesuvius, Pompeii and the ruins of the Greek temple of Paestum. Cut off from the north by the Sorrento peninsula extended by the rock of Capri, the bay of Salerno, surrounded by an amphitheater of hills planted with olive, eucalyptus and pine trees, is a huge bight over 30 miles long. It was in this heavenly landscape that the Allies had decided to try their luck: the British would land in the northern sector, not far from Salerno, and the Americans in the south. Between the two assault sectors there was an intervening stretch about seven miles long. The entire contingent was placed not under the command of Patton, who had been discredited for slapping a soldier on a hospital bed, but of US General Mark Clark.

In spite of surveillance of the air space, the *Luftwaffe* succeeded in spotting the 700 ships of the Allied armada (7 of which were aircraft-carriers) responsible for escorting, and also supplying firepower and transport for the 55,000 men in the first assault wave (including the Commandos and the Rangers). Actually this discovery came as no surprise: after all, it was the day after the capitulation of Italy and in Berlin, they were expecting some sly move on the part of the Allies precisely in the Gulf of Salerno, which was perfectly suited to an amphibious operation and situated, moreover, in the vicinity of the port of Naples within striking distance of the fighters based in Sicily. The whole business got off to a bad start, especially since General Clark, commander-in-chief of the operation, had ruled out prior bombardment of the coastal defenses in order not to give away the future assault sector to the enemy and also because the diversionary maneuver planned on Rome (parachute drop of General Ridgway's 82nd US Airborne Division) had had to be cancelled.

General Mark Clark, commander of the US troops in Italy. Ambitious, tough with his subordinates, hated by his soldiers – whose lives he did not hesitate to sacrifice – and indifferent to the difficulties experienced by his colleagues on the battlefield, Clark, unlike Eisenhower, was not a likable figure.

A German propaganda poster casting an ironic glance at the slow progress of the Allied armies inland from the peninsula. The Salerno landing was followed by the resignation of Mussolini and his replacement by Marshal Badoglio, who signed an armistice with the Allies and then joined their side.

Hardly had they left their landing craft than the attackers encountered serious resistance on all sides. On the evening of D-Day, the junction of the two assault sectors had not been obtained, the planned objectives had not been achieved and the beachhead was lacking in depth. This was the moment, when the enemy was at his most vulnerable, that the Germans launched a violent counter-attack. Faced with the incessant fire of the armored tanks from the 16th *Panzerdivision*, the Allied troops had to fight fiercely against the *Panzers* in the midst of ruins dating back to Antiquity, oleander bushes and orchards of almond trees.

Infantry in the mountains of the Italian peninsula.

SALERNE

In the Salerno sector, German troops are resisting in very tough combats against the British and US forces. "In Raum von Salerno stehen deutsche Truppen in erbittertem Kampf gegen Starke britisch-nordamerikanische Kräfte."

Die Wehrmachtberichte, 1939-1945

Convoy on an Italian road.

SARDINIAN MULES ACCORDING TO US WAR REPORTER ERNIE PYLE

"During the Italy campaign, the Allied battalions made great use of mules. They were the only animals capable of travelling along the narrow, stony mountain roads of the peninsula and transporting supplies to the front-line soldiers (cans of water, cases of ammunition and rations, radios, rolls of telephone wire, sacks of mail...). The convoys, with up to a hundred animals and led by requisitioned Sardinian mule skinners, left at nightfall to avoid coming under fire from the enemy's artillery. Behind the long line of mules was a second column of several hundred soldiers who went as extra carriers (clothes, packets of cigarettes, pharmaceutical products...) and helped with unpacking at the top. The return journey was more difficult, as the Italians refused to lead the mules loaded with the bodies of soldiers lying across the packsaddles, heads hanging down on one side and legs on the other; and the Americans were reluctant to put the bodies straight when they slid to one side or another."

Ernie Pyle, Brave Men

Crossing a village. The Italians extended a very warm welcome to the Allied troops.

On September 11, when casualties were beginning to reach devastating proportions and the situation was near-catastrophic, Clark sent out a cry of alarm and was beginning to contemplate a withdrawal, an evacuation of the beachhead.

In order to save Salerno, Eisenhower had to mobilize all his forces: he ordered the Navy to come in close to the shore and pound the German positions up to about twelve miles inland, and to land an extra tank division. All available resources in the Mediterranean theater of operations were requisitioned and allocated to transporting a regiment of the 82nd Division, along with equipment and engineers given the special task of constructing air-strips behind the beachhead.

Thanks to this general burst of activity, by mid-September the situation had been saved; the beachhead reached a depth of 12 miles at its maximum point and stretched across a front of around 45 miles. However, for a long time Clark still made little headway, sustaining considerable losses in the process. On October 1st, after three weeks of fierce fighting and eighteen days behind schedule, the Allies came in sight of Naples, but they had no intention of dying. Three months later, at the end of 1943 – in the Italian winter, in the rain and the mud that paralyzed progress towards the Gustav line – Clark was still more than 75 miles from Rome. "It's a long way to Rome," said German propaganda ironically! After coming so very close to disaster, the Salerno operation demonstrated the urgency, once a landing had been made, of losing no time, making quick progress, penetrating inland and gaining ground in order to put the beaches cluttered with equipment and the air-strips out of the range of enemy fire, whilst also attempting to link up the assault sectors. In short the maneuver was clear, a vigorous thrust was necessary to try to break out and create a single widened beachhead.

In order to release Clark's troops who had got themselves into a corner along the Tyrrhenian coast, and ease their progress up towards Rome, the commanders of the operation decided to launch a new assault against the rear of the German army, 35 miles further north, in the Anzio sector.

Flying Fortress. In the fall of 1943, the Allies intensified the strategic aerial bombardments on the towns and industrial centers of the *Reich*.

Anzio

Operation Shingle

January 22, 1944

Just as the objective of the Salerno landing, carried out against the rear of the German army, had been to assist Montgomery's troops, who had landed a few days earlier at the extreme southern tip of the peninsula, to break through northwards, the Anzio landing would enable the troops of General Clark blocked on the Gustav line of fortifications to resume their march towards the Eternal City. It had been hoped that, sandwiched between the two, the German 14th Army would give way. Comprising roughly 60,000 men placed under the command of the American General Lucas, the small Allied army landed at night on three beaches, on either side of Anzio and Nettuno, two small fishing ports approximately 35 miles south of Rome. The surprise effect was complete, and the landing was a success: in the first 24 hours, 35,000 men and more than 3,000 vehicles were brought ashore.

More preoccupied with consolidating the beachhead secured, landing the remaining men of his army and establishing a line of advanced defense of more than 20 miles in order to shelter the beaches from enemy fire than with making a thrust inland, General Lucas was to be surprised by the speed, violence and scale of the German counter-attack under the command of General Kesselring. By

THE TRAGEDY OF ANZIO

No landing in Europe or in the Pacific had greater success than that of Anzio-Nettuno. The losses sustained during the day of January 22 amounted to 13 killed, 44 missing and 97 wounded. The road to Rome, a city just 40 miles away, seemed open. On January 28, 1944, furious that the Wehrmacht had not driven back the attackers, Hitler sent a directive to the commander of the troops on the Italian front, General Kesselring, in which he gave his orders: "We will fight with fierce hatred against an enemy who is leading a merciless war of annihilation against the German people and who is contemplating the destruction of Germany... Der Kampf muss ein harter und erbarmungsloser sein." [The combat must be hard-fought and ruthless]

Transporting assault troops by LSI.

engaging the *Luftwaffe* forces in huge numbers against the concentrations of ships and launching a simultaneous counter-attack on land with mostly armored vehicles, the enemy pushed back the Allies, inflicting extremely heavy losses in the process. As at Salerno, three months earlier, there was a critical moment and once again, the intervention of the naval artillery and fighter-bombers was responsible for an almost miraculous recovery.

In the process, five thousand Allied soldiers had lost their lives or were wounded and Anzio, like Omaha later on, remains in American and British memories as one of the most furious and deadly battles of the war. For the strategists, on the other hand, Anzio is the example of a successful landing that was spoilt by the inability of the commanders to exploit their initial gains. The easily predictable outcome was that the Allied troops were confined in a pocket for long months, under fire from the German artillery. It was only on June 5, 1944 that the Allies, led by Generals Mark Clark and Alphonse Juin, entered Rome, the first liberated European city. But *der Fall von Rome* (the fall of Rome), a major event in the history

American troops landing on the beach in Anzio.

of the war, would be totally eclipsed by the Normandy invasion. In the following months, the Allied command would be dispossessed of its troops in the light of the Provence invasion, and would have to let the tough battle of Italy die a slow death.

Although costly in terms of human lives (over 300,000 men for the Allies, more than in the Normandy campaign, and 400,000 for the Germans, the same number of losses as in Africa, Stalingrad or Normandy), the Italian campaign immobilized 22 German divisions in

German prisoners (May 1944) captured by the troops of the French Expeditionary Corps.

the spring of 1944, compared with 8 on the eve of the landing at Salerno early in September 1943. If the 14 divisions that were thus neutralized in the Mediterranean peninsula had been on the western front, they could have spelled disaster for the Normandy landings. Just as the Allied operation in Sicily in July 1943 had relieved the pressure on the Soviet front and contributed to success at Kursk (Operation Citadel), likewise Salerno and Anzio played a part, if only an indirect one, in the Allied success in the Channel. This operation to come was certainly no foregone conclusion: after all, the shores of the Bay of the Seine were protected by the famous Atlantic Wall and defended by the *Wehrmacht*!

Canadian soldier protecting a friendly company patrolling at the bottom of the valley.

German sentry on the ramparts of the Atlantic Wall.

THE ATLANTIC WALL

"Hitler would invariably place the Atlantic Wall at the forefront of any assessment. Apparently indoctrinated by his own propaganda on the subject for so long and without having ever actually seen it for himself, he formed a mental picture of it based on the quantity of concrete that it had swallowed up, on the number of men working on it and on comparisons with the Maginot line fortifications."

Général Warlimont, "Inside Hitler's Headquaters"

The Atlantikwall

A linear defensive system on the model of the Maginot line, the day before the Allied operation in Normandy the Atlantic Wall comprised approximately 12,000 fortified works along the coasts of France. If we add to the concrete the thousands of guns and machine guns, the minefields on both land and sea, the hundreds of thousands of beach obstacles, the ditches and anti-tank walls as well as the flooded areas, we realize that the Wall was no mere bluff, as Marshal von Rundstedt would have had us believe, after the war.

A COLOSSAL BLUFF

"Er war ein ungeheurer bluff... [The Wall was a huge bluff], not so much for the enemy, who knew very well through his agents and from other intelligence sources, as for the German people. Hitler never saw the Atlantic Wall nor even any part of it..."

Statement by von Rundstedt during a post-war interrogation

Brest: a submarine base.

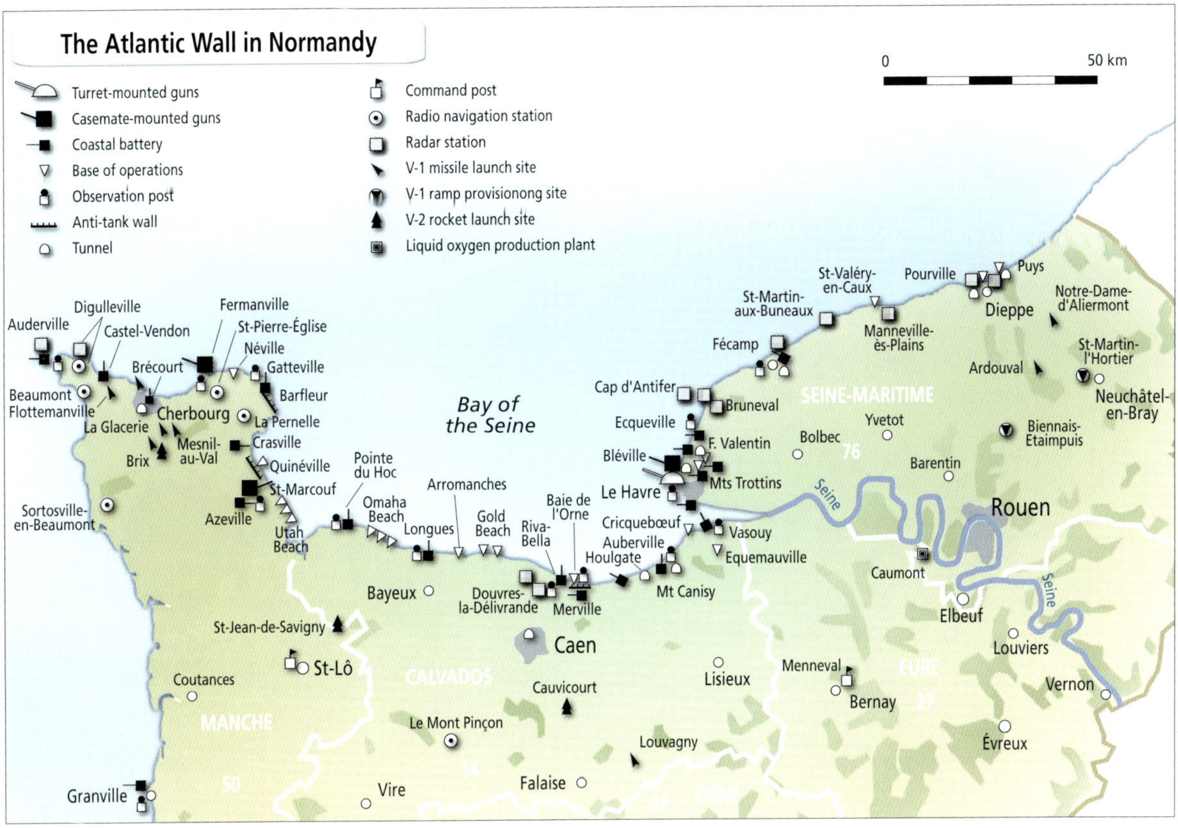

The Atlantic Wall in Normandy

The strength of the German defensive system was all the more surprising given that the first systematic work to place defenses along the coast of western Europe only started in the spring of 1942. Until this date, the biggest building sites opened by the German army on French territory were the five submarine bases at Lorient, Brest, Saint-Nazaire, La Pallice and Bordeaux and also various landing strips for the *Luftwaffe*. It was only towards the end of 1941, when the United States entered the war, that they started thinking in Berlin of putting up a defensive system along the coast. America's entry into the war increased the threat hanging over the rear of the German army, at that time wholly committed to the merciless struggle on the Russian front. In order to prepare for the danger of a landing operation to the rear of the *Wehrmacht*, Hitler then took the decision to erect a line of fortifications on the shoreline of western Europe from Friesland to the Spanish border.

In August 1942, a few days before the Allied operation on Dieppe, he fixed the number of *Verteidigungswerken* (defensive concrete structures) to be constructed at 15,000 and the number of men assigned to form the garrison of each bunker at 20. In a word, an army of 300,000 men would keep guard on the endless 2,500-mile stretch of coastline extending from northern Holland to Spain. German

Hitler and his generals: *"Rommel is applying all his intelligence to perfecting the fortified installations in the west [...] The* Führer *is absolutely certain that the invasion will fail."* (Goebbels, *Diaries*, April 18, 1944.)

Right page: German propaganda poster in Dutch designed to discourage the Allies from launching their amphibious operation.

propaganda christened this defensive line *Atlantikwall* (Atlantic Wall). However, contrary to what the term wall might convey, it was in no way a continuous obstacle protecting the *Festung Europa* (Fortress Europe) like ramparts surrounding a medieval castle. More like a fence or a string of pearls, the line of fortifications alternated strongholds with long sectors of lesser resistance.

Bearing more resemblance by its dimensions to the Great Wall of China than the Siegfried line or the Maginot line, the Atlantic Wall was to be the biggest building works undertaken by the Todt Organization (TO) in France between the spring of 1942 and the spring of 1944. For its completion, this imposing program had been divided up into several successive stages. The first and most important stage involved the fortification of those sectors judged to be most vulnerable (islands, large ports, submarine bases, river mouths, low gradient beaches suitable for an amphibious operation...). As regards the density of the structures to be built, the shore occupied by the 15th Army and extending from Le Havre to Antwerp was clearly a top priority. As we see, from the outset the German strategists had placed their bets on an Allied landing taking place north of the Seine rather than to the south and most probably in the immediate vicinity of a large port. The frontal assault carried out by the Canadians on Dieppe in August 1942 only made the German High Command even more convinced that the Allies were bound to need the installations of a large port in order for their operation to be successful. In blocking the main gateways to the continent when approaching from the sea by an accumulation of defensive means, the Germans were convinced that they had discovered the weak link in the Allied strategy.

UNAPPROACHABLE HARBOURS

"However, it is crucial that the enemy captures a port if he is to carry out a large-scale landing. This fact underlines the importance of the west coast ports. Accordingly, I have ordered that these ports be turned into strongholds."

Hitler, Führerbefehl [order from the Führer], January 19, 1944

ATLANTIK
WALL
1943
IS
GEEN
1918

Overlord, a disconcerting operation

In actual fact, by choosing to land deep in the Bay of the Seine, on a shore that was relatively distant from the English coast and therefore less heavily fortified and, moreover, on open beaches between the ports, the Allies succeeded in throwing the defenders off balance. Further disorientated by the steady stream of false information broadcast by the enemy under Operation Fortitude and taken up in the reports of Colonel Baron von Roenne, the German military, including Rommel, were led into thinking that the operation in Normandy was only a decoy and that they should expect the real invasion in the Pas-de-Calais. Even Hitler fell into the trap, until the end of July. Given the task of assessing the Allies' military potential and providing reports on the intentions of the Anglo-Americans, Colonel von Roenne received his information from a handful of German secret agents living in Great Britain. What he didn't know was that his informers, all identified by the British, were directly manipulated by the Intelligence Service. Not questioning the content of the messages he received, Roenne unwittingly proved to be an excellent go-between for Operation Fortitude and, just as the British wanted, he would provide exaggerated figures in his reports on the number of US divisions that were stationed in Great Britain and were about to cross the Channel. Using the threat of a second Allied operation in the Pas-de-Calais, he would encourage Hitler in his refusal to weaken the forces of the 15th Army! In short, Colonel von Roenne was an indirect architect of Rommel's failure in Normandy. A typical representative of the Prussian aristocracy in much the same way as von Rundstedt, Roenne would be sentenced to death in October 1944 for being one of the July 20 plotters.

A collection of decoys and all kinds of stratagems, Fortitude implemented on a vast scale all the usual methods of the secret services as well as numerous deceptions of its own, not to mention the key contributions of the French, Belgian and Dutch resistances. Apart from the extraordinary exploits of the Intelligence Service, what was most surprising in this operation was that so many high-ranking German officers had managed to be taken in by all the lies and ruses of the Allied strategy of deception.

Concreting a casemate for a medium-caliber gun.

The builder of the Wall

It was the Todt Organization that was assigned the task of building the Atlantic Wall. Although little known to the general public, this institution, one of the most effective under the 3rd Reich, was not on its first assignment of this kind. It had already built the motorways of the *Reich*, and the Siegfried line also called *Westwall* (Western Wall) on the western border of Germany.

After the start of the war, it was to the Todt Organization, which had by then become the agency responsible for carrying out the *Wehrmacht*'s construction projects, that the *Kriegsmarine* and the *Luftwaffe* would turn

Above:
Stamp on a Todt Organization pass.

Opposite:
Cover of a German propaganda document designed to show the similarities between Todt and Vauban in defending the French coastline against England.

Foreman with the brown uniform of the TO's officers.

TWO ADVERTISEMENTS PUBLISHED IN A FRENCH DAILY NEWSPAPER IN 1943:

Jobs available: joiners, carpenters, laborers. Good wage. Travel allowance. Company working for the occupying authorities. Tecnotramo, route de Paris, Champagne (Sarthe). V 1837, Le Mans.

German army seeks non-specialist workers, immediate start, for excavation work, Brest area. Interviews 24-26 August, 3-7pm. Café des Halles, rue de la Mairie, Brest.

for the building of submarine bases and airfields. After the invasion of Russia, the TO was called to the eastern front to repair roads and hydroelectric dams and adapt the railways to standard gauge. In the spring of 1942, after taking the decision to fortify the coastline of western Europe, Hitler appointed Speer, the new chief of the TO, to oversee the execution of the work. To execute the vast program of construction of the 15,000 bunkers within the deadlines set by the *Führer* (the main superstructure to be completed by May 1st 1943), the technical chiefs-of-staff representing the Todt Organization were to mobilize about 200 German civil engineering companies. After contracting various work to the TO, the German companies would in turn subcontract part of the work to French companies specializing in excavation work, concreting, road-building or digging underground works.

In order to gain time, the engineers of the TO placed a certain number of standard blocks at the disposal of the armies allocated to the shore defenses. Enabling the simplification of work order and estimates (volume of earth to be removed, supply of materials, labor requirements, construction deadlines...), standardization presented the additional great advantage of making it possible to envisage mass prefabrication of certain elements (concrete beams, armor-plated doors, electrical and telephone equipment, ventilation ducts...). This excessive standardization made the Atlantic Wall a repetitive and monotonous fortification made up of thousands of grey concrete blocks more or less sunk into the ground. A far cry from the fortifications in the style of Vauban!

In order to procure *Arbeitskräfte* (labor), at the start of the war the Todt Organization called upon volunteers; later, non-compulsory enrolment being insufficient, the occupying forces contrived with the complicity of the Vichy authorities to create unemployment in the French economy and requisitioned foreign workers such as the Spanish Republicans who had sought refuge in France. In order to attract French workers, the TO launched numerous propaganda campaigns based on the high wages and many bonuses available to volunteers taken on and also the guarantee that workers on the Atlantic Wall construction program would not be deported to Germany. According to the archives, in June 1944, the Todt Organization had 300,000 men working on its building sites throughout France. Out of this total, roughly a third were Frenchmen and the other two thirds were foreigners, especially Soviet partisans, Poles and Czechs, all considered as forced laborers. Treated like prison convicts, these men were condemned to mass-producing bunkers, fortified structures that would bear witness for a long time to come to the presence along the shores of France of a monster machine in the service of a wildly irrational cause.

Construction of a major Atlantic Wall installation. The concrete bars were positioned in three dimensions.

Long-range coastal defenses

With no navy or air force capable of providing seaward protection of the coasts of western Europe, the defense relied in June 1944 on a succession of artillery batteries scattered along the shoreline. We can estimate from German archives that at the moment of the Allied operation in Normandy, there were 800 gun positions on the shores of *Festung Europa* (Fortress Europe) with an approximate total of 3,000 guns.

The shore batteries were the most familiar elements of the Atlantic Wall and were the backbone of the coastal fortifications. These installations were allocated to the long-range defense of the shore, that is fending off an invasion fleet attempting to approach the

Over 95% of France's cement production was used by the occupying forces for the construction of the Wall.

Sangatte, the largest of the Wall's batteries (406 mm): *"A German film, 'The Atlantic Wall', is showing in a local cinema; it is most impressive. It is nothing but inaccessible fortresses, flamethrowers in action, elevators disgorging hundreds of foot soldiers armed to the teeth [...] How will the English get through?"* (Jean Galtier-Boissière, *Mon Journal pendant l'Occupation*, May 15, 1944.)

coast. Housing various pieces of artillery, a battery generally comprised four guns and a few subsidiary installations. The guns allocated to covering the sea had originally been placed on circular concrete platforms surrounded by a low wall. With the increasing number of air raids, although the positions were cleverly camouflaged, the Germans were obliged to shelter the guns inside casemates. A casemate was a big cube-shaped bunker with a window

German inscription on a wall of the Todt battery: *"One of the two of us will give in, and it will never be Germany."*

opening out towards the sea, and comprised a gun room where the gun was housed and, to the rear, one or two small rooms used as munitions stores.

Located ahead of the gun positions, the command post was usually on two floors: an observation post for the lookouts with field glasses on tripods, a map-room and telephone exchange on the ground floor and, upstairs, the range-finding post protected by a concrete canopy as at Longues-sur-Mer, near Arromanches, or open to the air as at the Pointe du Hoc. The link between the command post responsible for calculating firing coordinates and the artillery placed to the rear was obtained through underground telephone cables. Underground shelters used as barracks

Armored rangefinder.

Casemate with a medium-caliber gun responsible for the long-range defense of the shore.

for the garrison or ammunition stores were scattered around in the vicinity of the blockhouses. Defended by tank or machine gun turrets, by searchlights, ditches, minefields and barbed wire, each artillery position was an entrenched camp along the shore.

In order to equip its numerous coastal batteries, the *Reich* had salvaged pieces of artillery from all the arsenals of Europe. In this way, in the Bay of the Seine, between the Pointe de Barfleur and the Cap d'Antifer, around 40 batteries totaling a little over 150 guns were aligned along a 70-mile stretch of coastline. Among these, there were pieces of Russian origin at Ver-sur-Mer, Czech 210-mm caliber guns at Saint-Marcouf (behind Utah Beach) and at Merville (4 100-mm guns) and especially French guns taken from army stores, from the Maginot line or French coastal forts (old 194, 164, 155, 138, 120 or 95-mm guns). In short, weapons from a good half-dozen countries and of more than a dozen different calibers were used to defend the Wall. This wide variety of tubes made maintenance, spare parts supply, instructions for use and ammunition supplies a major headache and ruled out the construction of standardized gun positions.

Close-range beach defenses

Consisting of *Regelbauten*, or standardized blocks, the beach installations were very varied. The diversity of this category of bunker can be explained by the fact that it had to meet the many and varied requirements of the armies responsible for defending the shore (observation, transmission, detection, energy production, storage, repairs, shelters, firing...). Unlike the large shore batteries, the role of the beach installations was to ensure the close-range defense of the shore. These blocks, containing one or two gun slits and fitted with a small-caliber gun or machine gun, or with concrete niches topped with the turret of an old tank, were given the task of fighting off landing craft, armored vehicles trying to progress towards the beach exits or assailants who had set foot on land.

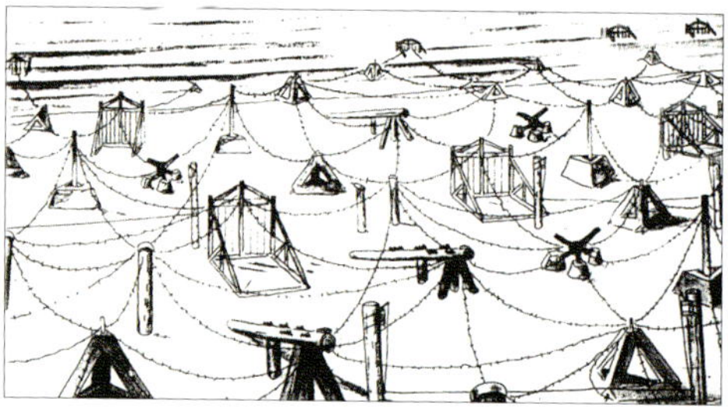

Picture of German beach obstacles.

Rails welded together and sealed in concrete blocks in order to tear open the assault craft.

Small installation for close-range defense. Below: Concrete niche topped with the turret of an old French tank.

The category of passive defense structures had an even more varied range of blocks. Among these were command posts often topped with an armored bell-shaped cover with a panoramic opening or fitted with a periscope emerging through the cover plate, telephone exchanges, radio stations, shops, workshops, ammunition stores and garages, and shelters for electricity generators (engine room, storage tanks, transformers...), for searchlights, for guns, for tanks... There were also shelters used as barracks for the troops (kitchen, mess, dormitory, infirmary...). The final type of passive infrastructure was made up of underground passages. In these vaulted, concrete tunnels, the same technical solutions were used to deal with water leaks, air replenishment and energy supplies.

The "wizards' war"

(Churchill)

It was vital for the defenders not to be caught by a surprise invasion. Hence the Germans had intelligence services in various neutral countries which from time to time sent reports and information regarding the Allied build-up, and also a line of radar stations along the coast of western Europe. Working on the principle that electro-magnetic waves are reflected when they come against an obstacle, these radar devices were available to give the alarm. The detection stations were fitted out by the *Kriegsmarine* or the *Luftwaffe* and installed at regular intervals.

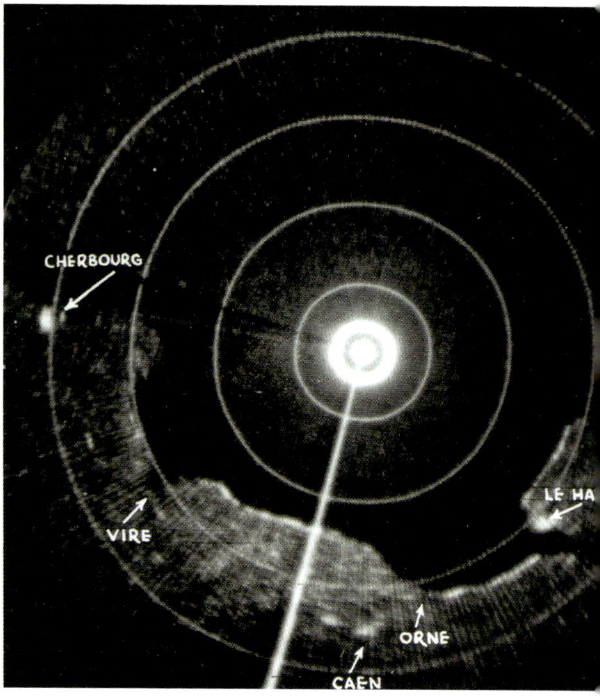

Superb image of the Bay of the Seine on an Allied radar screen.

Opposite: The *Freya* radar, a long-range detection device used by the *Wehrmacht* before September 1939. This device had a characteristic rectangular antenna for emission and reception.

Originally, from the summer of 1940 onwards, the Germans implemented two types of radar device along the Channel coast in connection with the Battle of Britain: the *Freya* and the *Würzburg*. With a range of around

The second-generation *Würzburg* radar (or *W. Riese*). Fitted with a parabolic antenna, the *Würzburg*, which used UHF waves, was positioned on a hexagonal concrete base. The antenna and cabin structure could turn through 360 degrees. With a range of 50 miles and range accuracy of 16 to 21 yards, this device, according to Anglo-American specialists, was *"one of the most well constructed and reliable of the war and even after the war"*.

Chain Home radar: the spectacular, immense metal pylon of a Chain Home Low station topped by a rectangular antenna similar to that of the *Freya*. The Chain Home Low devices, with a range of 80 miles, were specialized in the detection of aircraft flying at low altitude (below 10,000 feet).

65 miles, the *Freya*, with its characteristic rectangular antenna, was used for long-range exploration by both the *Kriegsmarine* and the *Luftwaffe*. Alongside this sentry, the *Wehrmacht* also had a second radar, the *Würzburg*, a detection device with a distinctive parabolic antenna. Developed by the firm *Telefunken*, the *Würzburg* was used by the *Luftwaffe* for automatically aiming anti-aircraft searchlights and guns and for radio-guiding fighters towards Allied bombers. Together these two electronic eyes, the one specializing in long-range detection, the other in close-range detection, gave the *Wehrmacht* a definite edge at the outset of war.

The lead gained by German technology in the field of detection was to be short-lived. The Allies had set their physicists to work on exploring a new direction, that of very high frequencies (VHF), and it was not long before they developed an electronic tube of unprecedented design, known as a "cavity magnetron". A genuine technological marvel, this generator of centimetric waves, capable of emitting very high levels of power, was one of the major discoveries of the Second World War. Moreover, it was small and meant that the radar could be miniaturized and installed on board airplanes, either for pursuit or for high-altitude blind bombing. The Germans discovered this lead gained by the Allies in early 1943, when

Mammut radar: as its name suggests, the *Mammut* was a huge radar with an immense rectangular antenna (33 x 100 feet), mounted on three pylons set on the cover plate of a bunker which housed the operators and radio-electric equipment.

Below: Constructed by the firm Siemens, the *Wassermann*, in its heavy version, was made up of several *Freya* antennae mounted on a 200 foot tall tubular mast, rotating on a steel stand sealed in the cover plate of the bunker. The transmitter was able to detect an aircraft flying above 5,000 feet, at a distance of 185 miles.

they shot down a British bomber in Holland equipped with a radar that had demanded more than a year of research to perfect by the teams of Allied scientists. This revolutionary device, code-named H2S, gave the navigator a panoramic screen on-board, which displayed an electronic picture of the ground being flown over! The German military could not believe their eyes! *"We had the shock of our lives at the beginning of 1943"*, admitted German specialists captured by the British, at the end of the war.

For the Reich, valuable time had been lost and the *Wehrmacht* would have to be content with improving the performance of the two basic appliances already available. From the *Freya*, an extremely cumbersome radar named

Mammut was devised, specializing in the exploration of naval space, along with a gigantic radar known as *Wassermann*. As for the *Würzburg-Riese*, a new, more high-performance version of the original *Würzburg*, a hundred of which would be installed by the *Wehrmacht* along the shores of France, it could raise the alarm to the fighters about ten minutes before the arrival of an enemy air formation, flying at speeds of around 340 mph. In all, it may be estimated that between Dunkirk and the Hague peninsula, there were more than a hundred detection devices, including at least fifteen early-warning radars (eight *Wassermanns* and around ten *Mammuts*) able to scan the sea and the sky above the Channel on a permanent basis. The *Wehrmacht* high command could feel safe.

Thin aluminum strips used to scramble German radars. These strips, 10 inches long and between half an inch and an inch wide, were launched in packs at the rate of one pack per minute so as to produce a white streak on the screen which would conceal the bombers. Known as "windows" by the airmen, the strips, one of the most effective weapons against the German defenses, were first used on July 23, 1943 during a bombing raid on Hamburg.

JAMMING

"It had been found that strips of paper with one side metallised, such as is often used to wrap up chocolate, were quite sufficient [...] to reflect radio waves strongly. [...] We hoped to be able to sow confusion among the German radars, as the false echoes produced by the strips, known as windows, would make it difficult to spot the devices themselves."

W. Churchill

If the Allies were to maintain the benefits of the element of surprise, a major factor in the success of a military undertaking such as that carried out in June 1944, the most dangerous stations of the Bay of the Seine had to be knocked out either by advance bombing raids or by an electronic jamming operation, while maintaining the basic principle: for every station destroyed in the future landing area, "*two outside it*" would be destroyed. The operation designed to blind the screens at the German detection stations would be carried out by a naval and air fleet during the night of June 5 to 6.

If we are to believe the post-war written account by Admiral Krancke, regardless of the general breakdown of the detection system, one radar station located to the east of Cherbourg (on the hills of La Pernelle), did make out at around 2.00 a.m., despite a recent bombing, that something unusual was going on in the western half of the Bay of the Seine and more precisely off Port-en-Bessin, without however being able to gauge the size of the target. Although coming on top of the numerous messages indicating that gliders and paratroops had landed in various parts of Lower Normandy since midnight, according to Krancke this warning was taken seriously neither by Marshal von Rundstedt, commander-in-chief in the western theater of operations, nor by General Speidel, deputizing for the absent Rommel as commander of Army Group B. After all, back in November 1943, hadn't Hitler dispossessed von Rundstedt of part of his command by relieving him of the preparation and conduct of the struggle against the Anglo-American invasion, appointing Rommel to this job? As for the phlegmatic Speidel, one of the officers who had joined the anti-Hitler resistance circle, during this decisive night he was to come round to the opinion of von Roenne who claimed that the Germans should stay where they were. He was encouraged in this wait-and-see attitude by the analysis of the previous amphibious operations carried out in Sicily and the Italian peninsula. During these last three landings, had not the Allies landed their troops in complete darkness? At three or four o'clock in the morning, nowhere had any landing on the Normandy beaches been reported. Keeping calm, Speidel refused to consider the situation to be serious even after the discovery by a German patrol, in the wreckage of a British glider, of a map that gave a fairly good idea of the scale of the Allied operation. Rommel's deputy would start wondering from 6.30 a.m., the time the seaborne landings began at Utah. Precious hours had been lost, and more vital hours were to be wasted waiting till the *Führer* woke up.

The Wehrmacht in the West

Like the Maginot line, the Atlantic Wall was an inert system. Designed to impede the attackers or slow down their progress inland, the concrete rampart alone was incapable of giving victory. This could only come from the intervention of the armed forces stationed behind the fortified complex. The outcome of the Allied amphibious operation depended not on concrete but on the power, scale and speed of the German counter-offensive. What then was the fighting potential of the *Wehrmacht*, the day before the invasion?

Comprising roughly 100,000 men, the German naval forces on the western front were placed under the authority of Admiral Krancke. Apart from the submarines, the German naval forces in June 1944 were incapable of putting up any serious resistance to the Allied navies. On the coasts of the North Sea, the Channel and the Atlantic Ocean, the *Kriegsmarine* had a few dozen ocean-going ships (destroyers, torpedo boats, patrol boats...) plus a handful of small units (merchant ships or fishing vessels converted into mine-sweepers...) responsible for protecting coastal waters. To these forces were added a few dozen submarines based in the West under Admiral Dönitz. At the time of the invasion, the action of the German naval forces would be fairly slight. Faced with the impressive array of resources deployed by the Allies, the submarine attacks were hesitant and uncertain. The torpedo-launches from Le Havre or elsewhere, on the other hand, turned out to be more aggressive.

Marshal Sperrle, formerly commander of the Condor Legion in Spain, was the leader of the *Luftwaffe* on the western front. A lover of fine food, living in a sumptuous castle in the Paris region where he enjoyed a luxurious lifestyle, Speerle was not in favor in Berlin.

With a wealth of human resources, the 350,000-strong German air force on the western front was placed under the authority of Marshal Sperrle commanding the 3rd *Luftflotte*. Just like the navy, in June 1944, the *Luftwaffe* was incredibly weak. Decimated by the British and American fighters, evicted from airfields

The 3rd *Luftflotte* was not able to defend the air space on the western front.

close to the coast, with a little under 1,000 aircraft the 3rd *Luftflotte* was unable to maintain air supremacy over France. However, after reinforcements arrived from the *Reich*, aircraft marked with the swastika did cause the Allies a few headaches after June 6 with their mine-laying activities each night in the Bay of the Seine.

With no navy or air force capable of bringing effective opposition to bear on the Allies, the defense of the shore rested almost exclusively on the shoulders of the land army. Although a million men were present behind the fortification besides another 450,000 marines and airmen, the army placed under the command of Marshal von Rundstedt was seriously flawed. Worn out by three years of war on the Russian front, the divisions suffered a cruel lack of means of transport (gun carriages, trucks), were partly composed of foreign units (*Osttruppen*) of doubtful patriotism and were equipped with an odd mixture of outdated weapons. According to General Zimmermann, von Rundstedt's chief-of-staff operations officer and the author of an interesting report on the war in the west, material shortcomings were not the most serious problem. This high-ranking German officer reserved his most biting criticism for the defective command structure, namely the excessive centralization of power in the hands of Hitler, the total absence of any coordination between the three services, and the overlap of skills.

The serious dispute between von Rundstedt and Rommel on the question of the stationing and use of the mobile reserve comprising about ten armored divisions was definitely a contributing factor towards the success of the Allied undertaking. This was the striking force of about 1,500 tanks that had been assigned the task of throwing the Allies back into the sea. Having failed to come to any agreement as to how to use the *Panzers*, the assault force ended up being split between the two commanders. This separation was to have disastrous consequences at the time of the invasion. Instead of a powerful offensive, the Allies had to face nothing worse than a series of isolated piecemeal attacks that they had no trouble in countering. With no clear strategy, the anti-invasion struggle was an undertaking that was doomed to failure.

***Osttruppen* or eastern troops. On the western front there were a number of battalions of foreign troops from the territories of the Soviet Union. The fighting value of these troops was mediocre and their loyalty left something to be desired.**

Marshals von Rundstedt and Rommel. These two men did not have the same views on the use of armored vehicles against an Allied invasion.

To this day, the philosophies of Rommel and of Rundstedt are the subject of lively debate. Who was right? It is possible to sketch a response to this question by examining what happened in Sicily, Salerno and Anzio. These experiences each demonstrated that the counter-attacks launched by the Germans against the Allied assault forces had been neutralized as a result of the support of the naval artillery and the fighter-bombers. Why would it have been any different in Normandy? Here, too, Rommel's lines of *Panzers* rushing for the beaches would have been the ideal targets for warships and the air fleet. Of course, this is all merely theoretical, but it is based on what took place earlier, at another moment during the war. It is clear that Rommel's strategy did not seem to be particularly ingenious, and it was probably von Rundstedt who was right: maybe the Germans would have had a better chance of success if they had attempted to defeat the invading forces inland, away from the firing range of the large naval craft.

Far removed from all these rivalries between their commanders, the troops maintained staunch discipline and remained confident. In certain units, as in the 12th SS *Panzerdivision Hitlerjugend* (25,000 men, twice the number of an infantry division), where morale was particularly high, the grenadiers could not wait to get the opportunity of measuring up to the Allies. In the Carentan sector, the American paratroopers of the 82nd and 101st Divisions would encounter fierce resistance from the young volunteer paratroopers of Colonel-Baron von der Heydte's 6th *Fallschirmjägerregiment* (parachute regiment). Two months later, when the military situation had worsened and seemed hopeless for the German 7th Army, half surrounded in the region of Falaise, General Schimpf commanding 3rd Paratroop Division did not hesitate to proclaim in a declaration broadcast to his troops that the Allied unit capable of capturing 3rd Division was not yet born! Indeed as it turned out, Schimpf walked away from all the ambushes that were set for him, and was to fight it out to the bitter end! Very different from such boasting was the atmosphere at supreme command level (in Saint Germain-en-Laye) and Army Group B command level (at La Rochefoucauld castle, in La Roche-Guyon, on the banks of the Seine) where Rommel responded to

Rundstedt's resigned indifference with pessimism and discouragement. In short, according to Zimmermann, the German western command had been overcome by the vague feeling that the situation was hopeless and that the combat to come was an unequal one.

Panzer in Normandy. On the eve of the invasion, Rundstedt wrote in a circular to be sent to the superior officers: *"Wo und wann der Angriff begint? wissen wir nicht."* (Where and when will the attack begin? We do not know.)

Aerial bombardment of Les Ponts-de-Cé, on the Loire, by the US Air Force.

THE OVERLORD PLAN

"Soldiers, Sailors and Airmen [...], you are about to embark upon the Great Crusade, toward which we have striven these many months. The eyes of the world are upon you [...] You will bring about the destruction of the German war machine, the elimination of Nazi tyranny over the oppressed peoples of Europe, and security for ourselves in a free world."

General Eisenhower's Order of the Day for June 6 1944

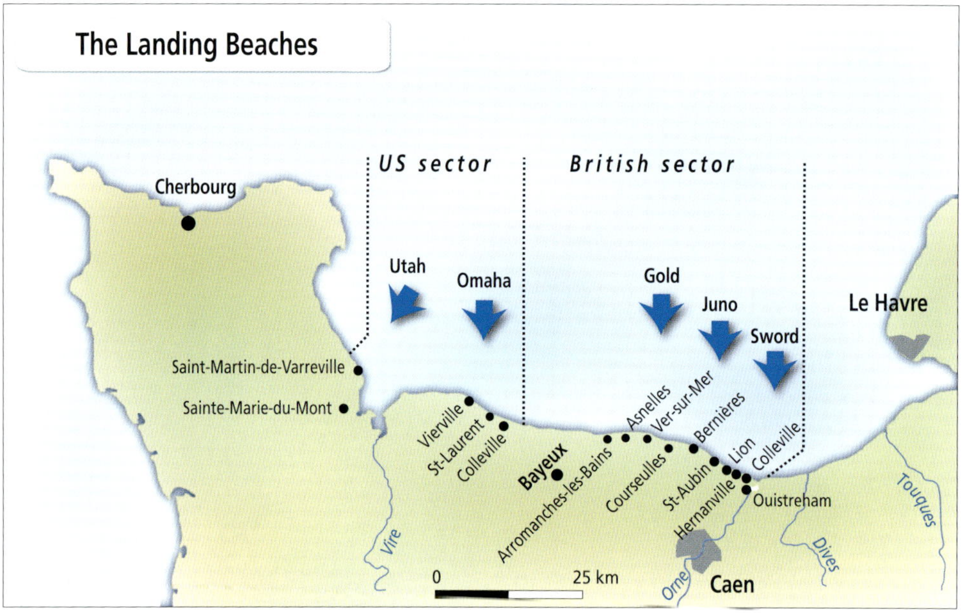

It was at the Quebec conference, in August 1943, that General Morgan, the chief-of-staff called upon to draw up plans for the big return of the Allied armies to the continent of Europe, exposed the broad lines of his project. Code-named Overlord, the operation, designed to push back the Axis forces and liberate the continent of the German occupation, envisaged a powerful attack in the Bay of the Seine, on the Normandy coast. Initially, the Allied assault was to be carried out early in May 1944 and to take place between the Orne and the Vire, on a front nearly thirty miles long, and three divisions were to be engaged. At the beginning of 1944, at Montgomery's request, the assault sector, considered to be too narrow, was widened. Thus, the invasion front first envisaged was extended to the west with Utah Beach, and to the east with Sword Beach. Out of the new total of five beaches, three were given to the British and the Canadians and

General Eisenhower, Supreme Commander of Operation Overlord.

Montgomery, commander-in-chief of the ground forces in Overlord, and Leigh-Mallory, commander of the air forces.

the two others to the Americans. Taken in its widest sense, the assault sector extended from Sainte-Marie-du-Mont to the Orne estuary, a distance of approximately 50 miles. The extension of the invasion front in turn demanded that increased numbers be engaged (three airborne divisions instead of two brigades and five infantry divisions instead of three). If we include the paratroops, the infantry and the sappers, it now became necessary to get 156,000 men ashore on D-Day. Introduced at the last minute, this increase in forces allocated to the initial thrust obliged Eisenhower, the Supreme Commander of Operation Overlord, to postpone the Normandy invasion until June 1st, 1944 in order to have another month in which to gather together the extra requirements in gliders and especially assault craft.

Why Normandy?

The first task that had to be resolved by COSSAC (the name of the Allied military staff responsible, from the spring of 1943, for drawing up the main outlines of the plan of the cross-Channel invasion operation) was to select an assault sector from the long stretch of shoreline extending from Denmark to the Spanish border. In order to make its choice, COSSAC took into account various elements such as the distance from the British airfields, the presence of a big port in the neighborhood of the assault sector, the existence of low gradient beaches, a hinterland likely to be suitable for the building of air-strips and for tank movement, and lastly, the strength of the Atlantic Wall shore defenses. Combining these different factors, COSSAC came up with a shortlist of two coasts, the Pas-de-Calais and the Bay of the Seine. Of the two sectors, the Pas-de-Calais unquestionably presented the greater advantages, but the strength of the German coastal defenses was such that the assault was in real danger of being transformed into a bloody disaster.

Various obstacles on Siouville Beach, in the Cotentin.

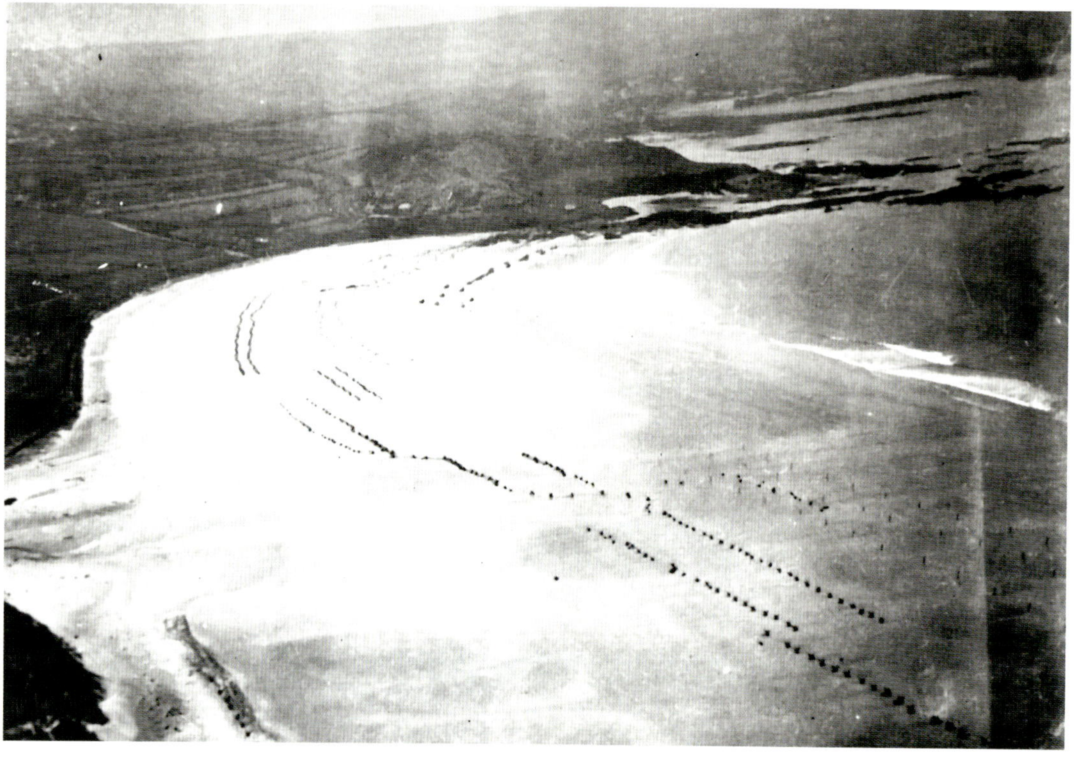

On the other hand, although much further from the airfields and ports of Britain, the coasts of Lower Normandy had a considerable advantage in that they could be cut off from the rest of France by destroying the bridges across the Seine and the Loire. Apart from this strategic edge, the shores of Lower Normandy were only lightly fortified, with long beaches protected from the prevailing winds by the Cotentin peninsula, and had two deep channel ports in Cherbourg on one flank and Le Havre on the other.

Destruction of the bridges over the Seine, here the metal bridge at Orival on the Caen-Rouen railway line. Almost 330 yards long, the bridge partially collapsed into the Seine on May 29, 1944, following an air raid.

Aerial photography

During the Second World War, aerial photography, which had already been used during the First World War, became very important as the main source of information about the enemy for the military staffs. For these aerial photography missions, in order to escape the enemy fighters, the Anglo-Americans used specialized squadrons of high-speed planes capable of reaching relatively high altitudes, including Spitfires, and later on twin-engined Mosquitoes or American Lightning fighters minus their heavy armament. With the increased speeds of the aircraft (300 to 375 mph), it became necessary to improve the performance of the cameras fitted under the fuselage or in the nose of the plane by improving the lenses, the quality of the films and especially the speed of the moving pictures. Depending on requirements, two types of photograph were produced. The more common type, the overhead photograph, was taken from an altitude of roughly 30,000 feet, and would later be used to produce topographical maps of the future invasion zone. In addition to overhead photographs, the commanders also required oblique angle pictures of the coastline. Taken from just above sea-level, roughly 3/4 mile off the Normandy coasts, such pictures provided an excellent view of the coast as seen from out at sea. When placed side by side, these large-scale (1/2,000) photographs gave a panoramic view of the coastline, enabling pilots on board the D-Day assault barges to find their way with ease and come ashore on the right beach. Thanks to high and low altitude aerial photography, whether overhead or oblique, the Allies had almost perfect knowledge of the coastline of the lower Seine and the hinterland, prior to the invasion. They knew the position of the enemy's large shore batteries, radar stations, anti-tank ditches and V.1 missile launching sites. Similarly, they had gained many vital pieces of information about

Photograph taken from on board a large US bomber with the standard US Air Force camera.

Longues battery (left to right): start of the construction (January 16, 1944), continuation of the work (March 27, 1944) and work near to completion (May 22, 1944).

the future field of battle: the breadth of the rivers, location of flooded areas, density and rate of flow of the communications channels, the whereabouts of impracticable sectors for armored vehicles and heavy materials, sectors suitable for setting up campaign airstrips, munitions dumps or fuel stores... Once the landing had taken place, aerial photographs would enable observers to monitor the progress of operations on land, spot the enemy's movements, obtain advance warning of enemy maneuvers, assess his weaknesses and reveal the extent of damage caused by the air bombardment. Specialists believe that this method supplied the command with more than three quarters of all intelligence obtained from the enemy. The other major sources of information for the Allies were Ultra (decryption of messages from the enemy), the secret agents in the resistance networks and the interrogation of captured prisoners.

Example of military intelligence provided by the Resistance in London. Drawn up by the Eleuthère network on January 9, 1944, this map depicts the Calvados coastline between Villers-sur-Mer and Deauville.

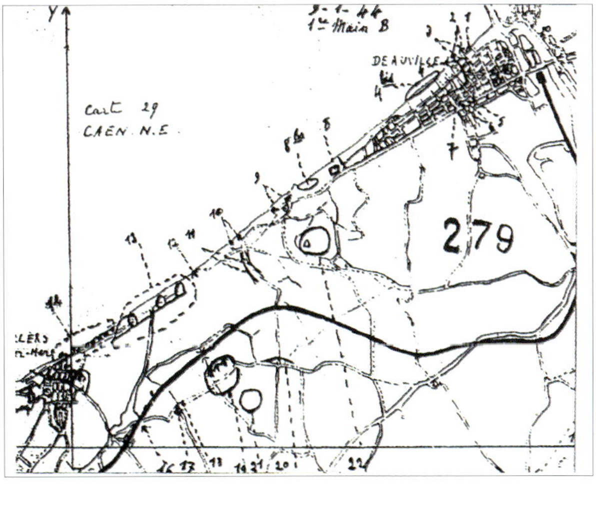

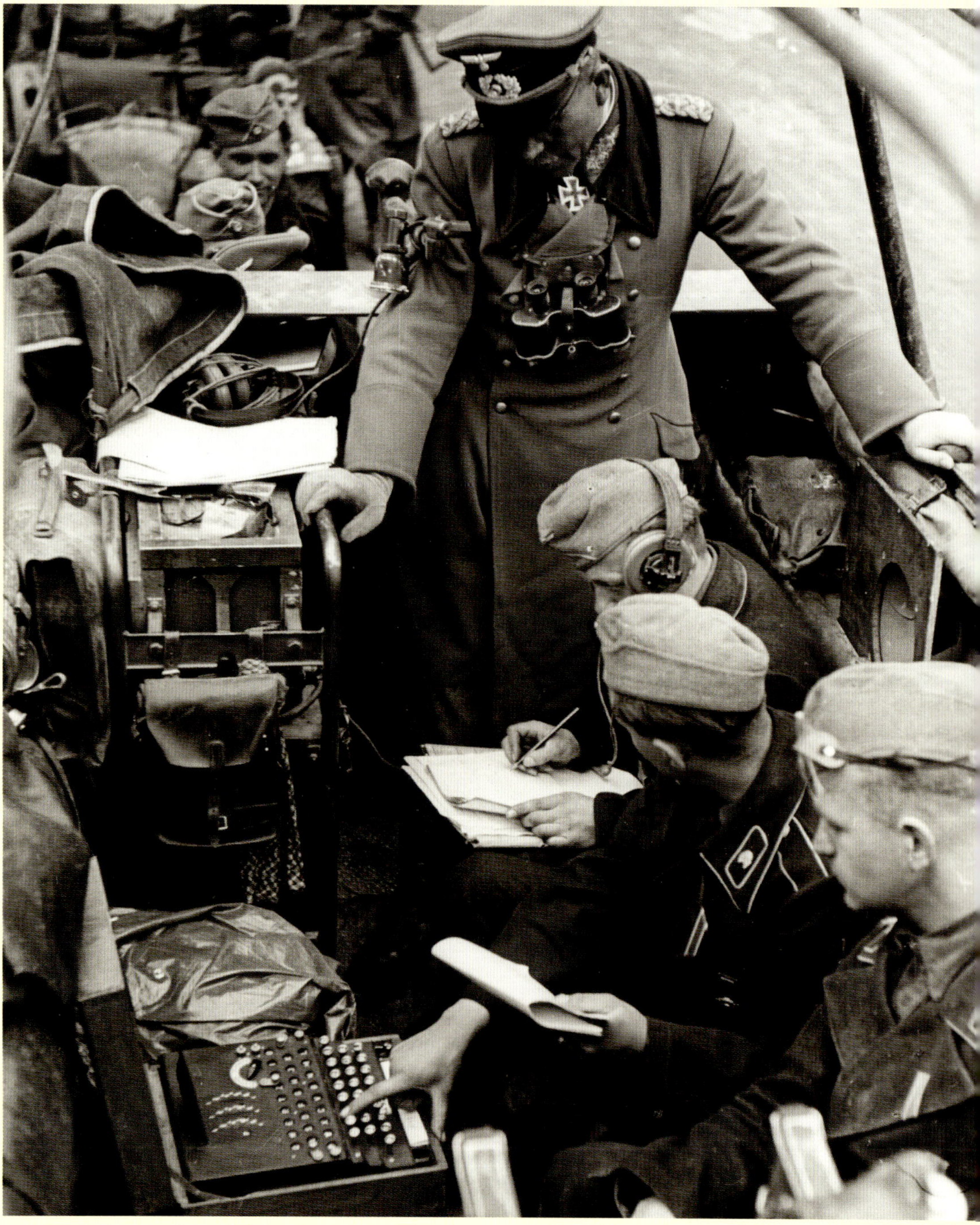

THE ENIGMA MACHINE

After having restored a machine used by the Wehrmacht to encrypt messages (a machine that was given to them by the Polish military intelligence services), the British – as unbelievable as it may seem – could access during the entire conflict the most secret instructions exchanged by radio between Hitler or the Oberkommando der Wehrmacht (the high command of the army) and the military staff of the armies on all the fronts! In order to distinguish them from other more traditional information sources, the messages from Enigma, the name of the German encryption machine, were given the name "Ultra" instead of the usual "Top secret". A new Delphic oracle, Ultra would prove to be exceptionally useful, both in the fight against the U-Boote (submarines), in the success of the Sicily and Italy invasions and in Operation Overlord. In Normandy, Montgomery and Bradley were able to confront the vicious counter-attacks because they were aware of their preparation. According to Eisenhower, out of all the factors that contributed to the final victory, none was as decisive as the breaking of the most secret codes of the enemy by the codebreakers at Bletchley Park: "Ultra was decisive."

Opposite: **Enigma machine on the French front in 1940.**

Final preparations

Whilst British and American shipyards had become an incredible hive of activity, building assault craft and sections of the artificial harbors, in early spring of 1944, the Allied air force began a vast bombing campaign against the road and rail communications networks in north-western France. This campaign was aimed at destroying bridges and tunnels, railways and sorting stations... in order to paralyze the traffic and delay the arrival of German reinforcements on D-Day to the future beachhead. At the same time,

Interpretation room for aerial photographs (US Air Force).

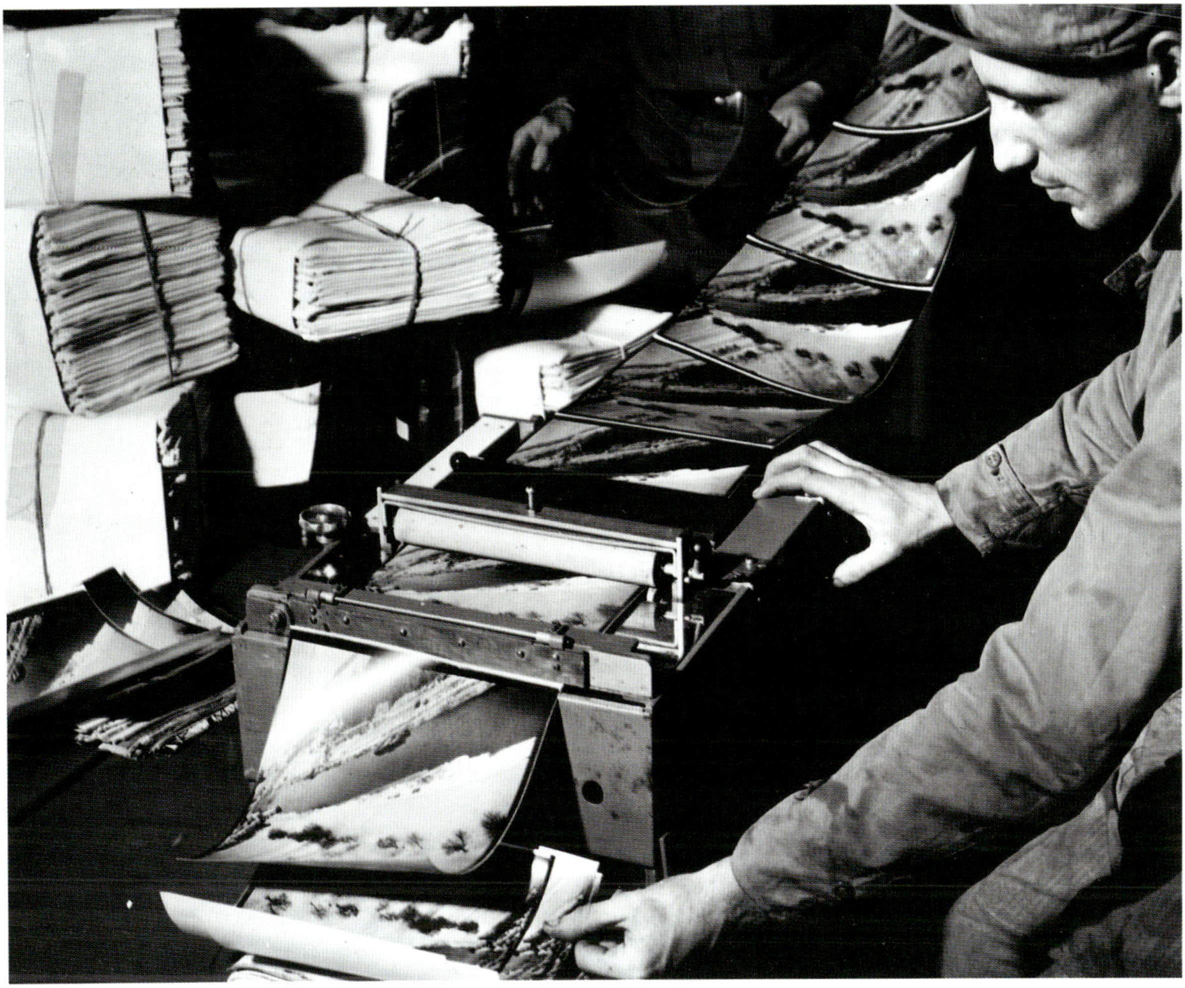

Guillotine automatically cutting a roll of aerial photographs printed by machine in less than five minutes.

the big bridges across the Seine and, subsequently, the Loire were bombed in order to isolate Brittany and Normandy from the rest of France. In April, a bombing campaign was begun against the coastal defenses of the Atlantic Wall. Between April 10 and June 5, 2,500 Allied aircraft took part in attacks against the coastal installations situated in the future assault zone. In order to avoid revealing the chosen objective, 6,300 sorties were also aimed at targets outside the invasion sector. During this period, Allied aircraft carried out a total of nearly 9,000 flights and dropped 23,000 tons of explosives on the coastal fortifications along the Atlantic Wall. In these final months, in Britain, the land forces detailed to lead the assault organized numerous exercises and, by spring, each man knew what it was to attack a beach in a landing craft with bullets flying in all directions and shells exploding at close quarters. The paratroops of British 6th Airborne Division, for their part,

Formation of Allied bombers above France.

B17 "Flying Fortress" bombers.

had reconstituted in close country in England an exact replica of the Merville battery, one of their objectives during the night of June 5 to 6, on the basis of indications supplied by air photographs. Similarly, as soon as he was briefed as to his objective, to capture the battery at the Pointe du Hoc, Colonel Rudder, commanding the 2nd Ranger battalion, was off training on cliffs of the Isle of Wight. Never had an amphibious operation been prepared so methodically and precisely, nor concealed with such intelligence and cunning.

Fortitude: an elaborate deception plan

In order to draw the attention of the defenders of the beaches away from the Bay of the Seine, a plan of deception had been laid by the Allied secret services for the German high command. Grouped under the code-name "Fortitude", the diversionary activities devised by London were twofold: Fortitude North was designed to mislead the enemy into believing that the Allies were building up for an invasion of Norway, and Fortitude South that the invasion sector was to be the Pas-de-Calais. So as to increase fears that the landing would take place in Norway, in the region of Trondheim, the Anglo-Americans concentrated ships in the north-eastern ports of Britain, began mine-laying operations in the waters of the North Sea and the Baltic and set off a series of attacks against the submarines off the coasts of Norway. As regards the Pas-de-Calais

Fake guns designed to deceive enemy aerial photographic reconnaissance.

sector, where the Germans were expecting the invasion to take place, they piled up various sections of the artificial harbors in the ports along the eastern coast of England facing Boulogne, carried out numerous bombing raids against shore batteries between Dieppe and Dunkirk as well as laying mines at both ends of the Straits of Dover and placing the French and Belgian resistance movements on the alert. Further inland, again with the intention of strengthening the convictions of the German high commanders, they turned out whole squadrons of dummy military equipment including inflatable rubber trucks, tanks and jeeps and also dummy airfields for wooden planes. All these measures were designed to contribute to fostering a climate of uncertainty and misleading the enemy. In May 1944, in one of the last of his weekly reports, von Rundstedt clearly stated that the sector under the greatest threat was unquestionably the coastal area to the north of the Seine. What is much worse, events would subsequently show that as late as the end

The inflatable rubber tank was another decoy.

A fake truck, part of the Fortitude equipment.

of July 1944, both Hitler and Rommel were still convinced that Overlord was no more than a diversionary operation and that the real invasion would take place in the Pas-de-Calais, hence the *Führer*'s adamant refusal to weaken his defenses along the front north of the Seine in order to strengthen the troops in Normandy. Intended to blind the enemy, Operation Fortitude continued throughout the night of June 5 to 6, with the dropping of dummy paratroopers in the region of Yvetot (near Rouen), Maltot, south-west of Caen, and Marigny, near Saint-Lô. During this famous night, again with the intention of deluding the German command, the Allies simulated the approach of a vast invasion fleet on the screens of the radar devices installed by the enemy between the Cap d'Antifer and Fécamp (Operation Taxable), in the Boulogne region (Operation Glimmer) and off Barfleur. At the same time, a fleet of 262 ships packed with electronic jamming equipment was detailed to neutralize German remote detection devices positioned in the Bay of the Seine.

At high tide or at low tide, by day or by night?

If a moonlit night was the obvious choice for the launching of the biggest military operation of all the time, insofar as the aircraft and glider pilots would be able to find their objectives, on the beaches, both night and day assaults had their supporters. At the top, this controversy was the subject of fierce argument between General Montgomery, commander of the land forces, who favored an initial attack at high tide and, above all, under cover of darkness, as in Sicily and in Italy, and Admiral Ramsay, who advocated

Supreme military staff of Operation Overlord, in Southwick Park.

Mined piles on a Normandy beach.

a daylight assault. After much discussion, it was finally decided to mount a dawn assault because of the risks of collision between the hundreds of craft pressed up against each other along the beaches and at the insistence of the naval artillery responsible for neutralizing the German coastal defenses. As for the choice of tide, it was the visibility of the obstacles planted on the beaches, between the low and high tide marks, that would settle the question. In order that the landing craft should not be ripped open by the lethal mines on top of inclined stakes, the landings would have to take place at low tide or on a gently rising tide. This double constraint restricted the dates available for D-Day: there are not many days a month when the tide is low just a few minutes before daybreak. Given the tidal conditions in the Bay of the Seine, it was arranged for the assaults to be staggered in time starting with Utah Beach and ending with Sword. As to the day that would see the start of the biggest amphibious undertaking in history, it was originally set for June 5, which left the 6th open as an alternative to fall back on, and the 7th another possibility. After postponing the operation for 24 hours due to bad weather, Eisenhower took the

Last meal on the transport boat before the assault.

historic decision on Sunday June 4, around 9.15 p.m., in the library of Southwick House in Portsmouth, which for several months had been used for Admiral Ramsay's headquarters. A few hours later, the thousands of ships making up the liberation armada, the biggest fleet that any Admiral ever had under his command, set off towards the coasts of Lower Normandy. Despite the fact that several amphibious undertakings had previously been carried out in the Mediterranean and the Pacific, no operation in any theater of war had come anywhere near the complexity of the Normandy landings. In Africa, Torch had been mounted against undefended and not entirely hostile shores. In Sicily and in southern Italy, the Allies had landed on non-tidal shores that were lightly fortified and encountered only token resistance from the Italian units. Anzio had taught nothing new, except to confirm the supporting role that the naval firepower could provide for the newly-landed troops. In the Pacific, the landings mostly took place on isolated islands and always during the day, at the request of the US Navy who insisted on being able to see the targets to be bombed.

Although valuable lessons had been drawn from all these experiences, the invasion in Bay of the Seine remained largely an unknown quantity: was it not against shores where the tides were of great amplitude, in a region with extremely changeable weather conditions, with beaches obstructed by murderous obstacles and closed off by walls or anti-tank ditches and swept by rapid fire from guns hidden in small pillboxes? As Eisenhower would later stress, the outcome was by no means a foregone conclusion. This is why, in order to break through this section of the Atlantic Wall, over a total length of 50 miles, the Allies had gathered together a formidable striking force including 7,000 vessels, 11,000 aircraft, 160,000 men and 20,000 vehicles.

The *Sten*, the weapon of the Maquis.

An act of sabotage on a railway.

Under such an onslaught, from the early hours of June 6, the most gigantic fortification of all time – according to German propaganda – collapsed. Chronologically, the June 6 operation can be divided into three stages: the airborne landings, the aerial and naval bombardments, and the seaborne landings with craft running up onto the shore.

THE WEATHER ON D-DAY

4th June. We met at 4 a.m. at Southwick House. Some of the convoys had already sailed, working to a D-Day of the 5th June. The weather reports were discouraging. The Navy reckoned the landing was possible but would be difficult. [...] Weighing all the factors, Eisenhower decided to postpone D-Day for 24 hours; it would now be on the 6th June.

5th June. We met at 4 a.m. [...] The Met. reports indicated a slackening of the storm and a period of reasonable weather on the 6th June... On that, Eisenhower decided to go. We were all glad.

B. L. Montgomery

AUTUMN SONG IN TOURCOING (JUNE 1944)

The SOE (Special Operations Executive), a branch of the British secret services responsible for carrying out sabotage in the rear of the German army in occupied Europe, had notified the leaders of the French Resistance that they would be informed of the start of the invasion by a BBC broadcast of two lines from the Verlaine poem entitled "Chanson d'automne" (Autumn Song). The first coded message would be broadcast on the 1st or 15th of the month in which the Allied operation would take place. The second line, "Blessent mon coeur...", would indicate to the Resistance that the invasion would take place within 48 hours of the broadcast and would give the order to start the planned sabotage operations (railways, pylons, roads, bridges...) in order to paralyze the enemy's movements.

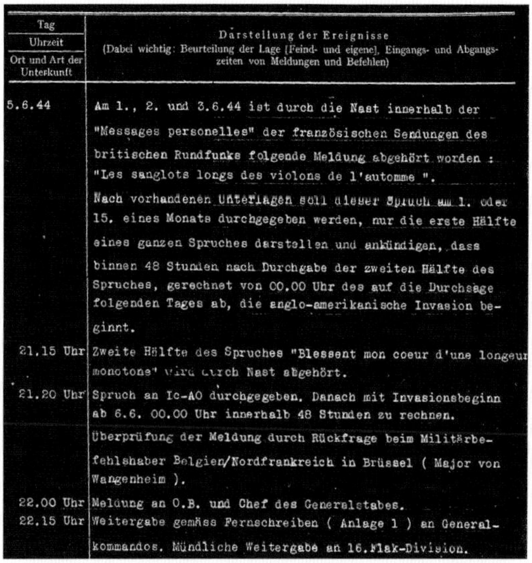

Tag / Uhrzeit / Ort und Art der Unterkunft	Darstellung der Ereignisse (Dabei wichtig: Beurteilung der Lage [Feind- und eigene], Eingangs- und Abgangszeiten von Meldungen und Befehlen)
5.6.44	Am 1., 2. und 3.6.44 ist durch die Nast innerhalb der "Messages personelles" der französischen Sendungen des britischen Rundfunks folgende Meldung abgehört worden : "Les sanglots longs des violons de l'automme ".
	Nach vorhandenen Unterlagen soll dieser Spruch am 1. oder 15. eines Monats durchgegeben werden, nur die erste Hälfte eines ganzen Spruches darstellen und ankündigen, dass binnen 48 Stunden nach Durchgabe der zweiten Hälfte des Spruches, gerechnet von 00.00 Uhr des auf die Durchsage folgenden Tages ab, die anglo-amerikanische Invasion beginnt.
21.15 Uhr	Zweite Hälfte des Spruches "Blessent mon coeur d'une longeur monotone" wird durch Nast abgehört.
21.20 Uhr	Spruch an Ic-AO durchgegeben. Danach mit Invasionsbeginn ab 6.6. 00.00 Uhr innerhalb 48 Stunden zu rechnen.
	Überprüfung der Meldung durch Rückfrage beim Militärbefehlshaber Belgien/Nordfrankreich in Brüssel (Major von Wangenheim).
22.00 Uhr	Meldung an O.B. und Chef des Generalstabes.
22.15 Uhr	Weitergabe gemäss Fernschreiben (Anlage 1) an Generalkommandos. Mündliche Weitergabe an 16.Flak-Division.

Copy of the page from the *KTB* of the *AOK 15* (war diary of the 15th Army) for the night of June 5 to 6.

Unfortunately, as Pierre Nord explains in his work My Comrades are Dead (Librairie des Champs-Elysées, 1947), the Abwehr (the German intelligence service), which had placed a great many informers in the Resistance movements since early April 1944, was aware of the meaning of the two coded messages broadcast by the BBC after the French-language evening news. The first line was picked up on the evening of June 1st by the permanent listening service tuned to British radio (NAST) that was set up in a large bunker in Tourcoing, and was transmitted to Oberst (colonel) Helmut Meyer, intelligence officer (IC in German military language) to the military staff of the 5th Army commanded by General von Salmuth. This alert, yet another one, was not taken seriously by anyone, and Rommel, Head of Army Group B, went to Germany on leave. When the second part of the message was broadcast on June 5, shortly after 9 p.m., Meyer once again alerted his direct superior, General von Salmuth, who, at the insistence of his intelligence officer, took the decision to alert the 15th Army, located north of the Seine. Apparently, no one thought to warn the 7th Army, the one responsible for defending the Normandy coast.

Cover of the *Kriegstagebuch* (war diary or *KTB*) of the 15th German army stationed in the north of France. Every day, in this register, all the incidents taking place in the sector of the army, along with all telephonic communications and telexes received or sent, were recorded.

"United we are strong, united we will win."

JUNE 6, 1944
OPERATION OVERLORD

"Our anti-invasion troops are all ready.
Let them come!"

Goebbels, Diaries, 18 April 1944

"Under the command of General Eisenhower, Allied naval forces, supported by strong air forces, began landing Allied armies this morning on the northern coast of France."

Official Communiqué No. 1, from Supreme Headquarters, Allied Expeditionary Forces.

The airborne landings

The assaults launched from the air marked the start of the large-scale operation. Performed at either end of the invasion zone, the objective of the parachute drops was to protect the seaborne offensive along its flanks. In the eastern sector (in the region of Ranville), the 6th Airborne Division under General Gale landed by parachute. Apart from the mission to protect the

Horsa glider being towed.

June 5, 1944, Greenham Common airfield. General Eisenhower visited American paratroopers before they left for Normandy.

British paratrooper during training.

Opposite: Final instructions before the jump above Normandy.

Towing a glider.

Opposite: British gliders landed near the Bénouville Bridge.

beachhead against any counter-attacks launched by the German 15th Army, the 6th Division was to capture the battery at Merville and the bridges on the shipping canal from Caen to the sea and on the Orne, and to destroy various crossing places on the Dives in order to hinder any counter-attack. On the opposite flank, in the Cotentin (in the region of Sainte-Mère-Eglise), the parachute landings were carried out by 82nd and 101st Airborne Divisions. Here again, these elite American troops were to capture certain fortifications or roads that had not been flooded and also destroy certain bridges. Due to wind, cloud, the violence of the German *Flak* (or *Flakartillerie*, a unit of anti-aircraft batteries), sudden evasive action taken by the pilots, and the flooded areas themselves, these airborne operations resulted in devastating losses.

The aerial and naval bombardment

The pounding of the artillery positions by the Royal Air Force (RAF) and the US Air Force had begun at the start of April. During the night of June 5 to 6, 2,500 bombers would drop nearly 8,000 tons of explosives on the ten largest batteries in the future assault zone. Due to a dense layer of cloud, the bombings produced very uneven results, particularly in what was to be the Omaha sector. In addition to the disruption caused to the artillery positions by the creation of numerous craters (to this day clearly visible at the top of Mont Canisy or the Pointe du Hoc) and the destruction of underground communications cables, the terrific explosions had a definite effect on the morale of the garrisons shut up inside the concrete blockhouses. At dawn, taking over from the air force, the naval artillery entered the fray. With this intention, a bombing fleet consisting of cruisers, battleships, torpedo boats and destroyers had taken up position facing the shore, on the morning of June 6. The bigger ships were placed on either flank of the sector opposite the more powerful batteries at La Pernelle and Saint-Marcouf to the west, Houlgate, Canisy and Le Havre to the east. The firing began at daybreak, half an hour before the troops were due to land. At that moment, it was light enough for observers in spotter planes circling above the German positions to

The HMS *Belfast* cruiser facing the Normandy coast. On the morning of June 6, the *Belfast*, with its 406-mm guns able to send an 1,800-pound shell 33,000 yards, would fire on the coastal battery of Houlgate and then on the city of Caen.

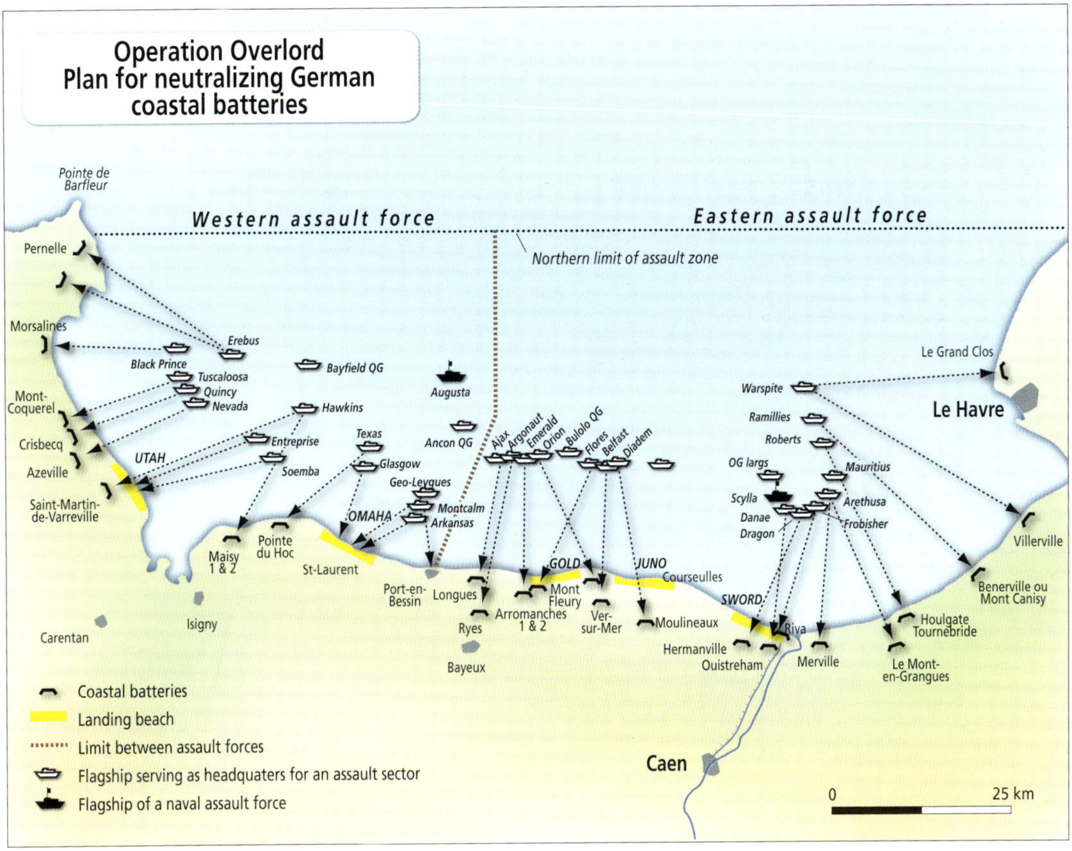

direct and correct the aim of the warships' large guns. The results of the naval bombardment were spectacular although they were unable to silence the shore guns once and for all. However unbelievable it may seem, the coastal batteries failed to hit a single large Allied unit taking part in the naval bombardment! On D-Day, the landing craft had more trouble with underwater mines, beach obstacles and maneuvering errors than with the poundings of the shore batteries. There was at any rate an overwhelming disproportion between the hundreds of thousands of tons of concrete that had been poured along the seafront to protect the Atlantic Wall artillery emplacements and results obtained in the final showdown.

Radar screen on board a bomber.

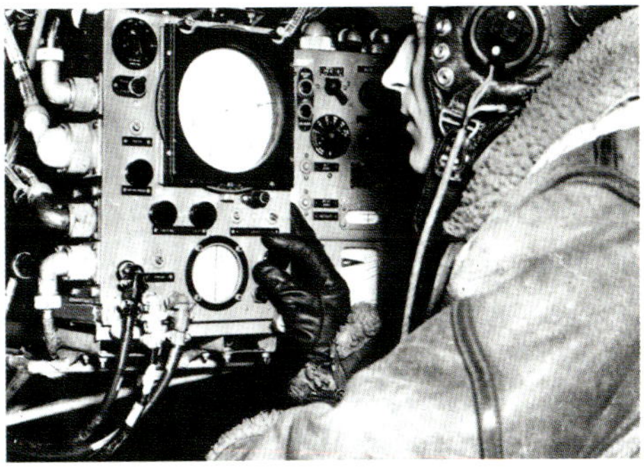

SPECIAL PRESS RELEASE

"June 6th. Special communiqué! The long-awaited British and American attack against the northern coast of France commenced last night." [...] The battle against the invading troops is raging."

Communiqué from the Wehrmacht on Berlin radio

Observation of the naval artillery fire on the German defenses.

The seaborne landings

Utah

Due to variations in the times of the tide, the seaborne landings were to be staggered, starting in the west at Utah and moving gradually eastwards to Sword. The mission entrusted to the US 4th Infantry Division (General Barton) was to establish a beach-head on the eastern seaboard of the Cotentin (Utah Beach), and to link up with the air-borne units and with those who had landed at Omaha. Their next objective was to cut off the Cotentin peninsula from the rest of France, capture the port of Cherbourg and break out towards the south. On Utah, the assault was going according to plan and by the evening of D-Day, a firm lodgement had been secured and there were few casualties. However, although enemy resistance had been relatively weak, at midnight the division had not achieved all its objectives.

The Pointe du Hoc

To prevent the American soldiers, who were landing on Omaha beach, coming under fire from the German artillery battery located close by on Pointe du Hoc, a Rangers unit was sent to neutralize the position before the troops reached land.

The attack was launched early on the morning of June 6, following the landing of a small troop at the foot of the cliff. Using rocket guns, the soldiers fired rope ladders attached to grapnels onto the ridge so they could climb up the cliffs. Despite the enemy defense, 150 Rangers reached the top of the cliff twenty minutes later and engaged in ruthless combat with the German gunners, who were hidden in the many underground passageways. However, the attackers only found wooden stakes on the concrete platforms and in the casemates, not artillery. Following the never-ending aerial bombardments, the artillery had been moved to a small lane one kilometre inland.

The Rangers found and blew up the six cannons, and settled in defensive positions to prepare for the arrival of the German rein-forcements. Along with the raids launched on Ranville bridge and Merville battery by the British paratroops on the night of June 6, the Pointe du Hoc attack was one of the most extraordinary feats of D-Day.

The task entrusted to the US 1st Infantry Division (General Huebner) was to establish a beachhead code-named Omaha between the Vire and Port-en-Bessin, then to head off south in the direction of Saint-Lô whilst at the same time deploying so as to link up with the neighboring beach forces of Utah and Gold.

Opposite: Pointe du Hoc after being captured by the Rangers (June 7 or 8). Top, sentries keep a close watch on a group of prisoners. They are most likely Polish prisoners (there were a number of them in the Pointe du Hoc garrison), who were forced to join the *Wehrmacht*. They fled during the attack and hid in the area around the battery. Center, a group of Rangers resting near the opening of a former underground tunnel. The concrete end was blown up or destroyed by naval bombardments. Finally, the photo shows that the Rangers did not attack the German coastal battery head on (at the foot of the firing station) but from a slight distance on the upstream cliff. An attack was also planned on the downstream cliff but, due to losses in the rough seas early on June 6, Colonel Rudder had to abandon this assault.

Assault fleet off Utah.

Omaha

The assault on Omaha was to encounter many difficulties and came very close to total disaster. It was only in late morning that the Americans got a firm and definitive foothold on the beach, with the arrival of extra reinforcements and a final surge of bravery. In the afternoon, when German resistance began to weaken owing to a lack of adequate reserves, the attackers managed to break through the line of coastal defenses and capture the village of Vierville. Meanwhile, the sappers cleared the beach of obstacles, filled in the ditches and cleared exits towards the hinterland. At the cost of appalling losses, the Americans had finally won the day.

Mined pile on Omaha Beach.

Gun in a casemate raking the beach.

Landing craft approaching Omaha Beach.

On Omaha, the fighting was fierce and bloody.

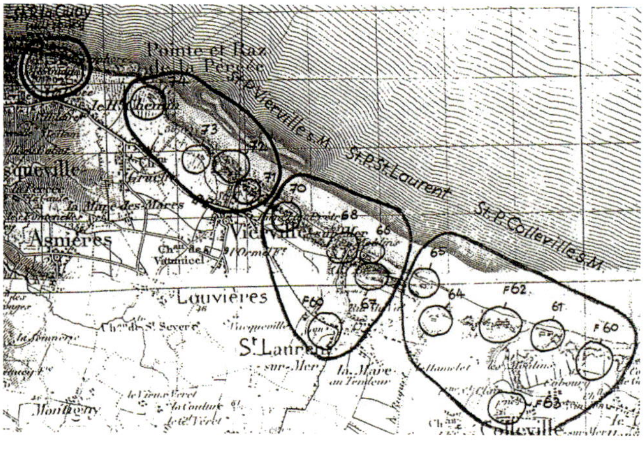

Opposite: Map showing German defenses on Omaha Beach. The four miles of beach had around fifteen *Widerstandnesten* (WN or nests of resistance) grouped into three bases of operations, or *Stützpunktgruppen*. Each WN was made up of small concrete forts armed with anti-tank guns, machine guns, turrets of armored vehicles set on a stone base, grenade launchers and flamethrowers. The defensive positions were linked by trenches. To carry out their shoreline fortification work, German engineers made extensive use of the French topographic map, with a scale of 1:80,000. A good example of this can be seen here with the location of the defences for the future 7 km long Omaha Beach.

One of the conditions for the success of the Allied amphibious operation was having control of the airspace.

Gold

To make a success of the assault on Gold Beach was the task of the 50th British Division (General Graham). Its mission was to create a vast perimeter with a view to putting the future artificial harbor at Arromanches out of range of the German artillery, and afterwards to link up with the Canadians from Juno. In spite of fierce resistance from the fortified emplacements at Le Hamel and La Rivière, the attackers managed to occupy the hills over the future mulberry at Arromanches as well as the heights above Port-en-Bessin. In this port, in the very heart of the assault area, the Allied command had decided to set up an oil terminal which was to supply the entire expeditionary force. By evening on June 6, having established a firm foothold on the continent, the 50th Infantry Division had succeeded in joining up with the Canadians of Juno Beach.

The Union Flag flies over Gold Beach.

The village of Ver-sur-Mer located behind Gold assault beach.

Landing on Juno Beach.

Juno

The 3rd Canadian Infantry Division (General Keller) was given the task of disabling the coastal defenses in the Courseulles-Bernières sector, then breaking out into the interior in the direction of highway 13 and Carpiquet airfield, whilst also deploying to form a continuous beachhead with the British from Gold Beach to the west, and Sword to the east. In spite of severe losses in landing craft caused by mined obstacles covered by the tide, the 3rd Division captured Courseulles and headed off towards the interior. They soon encountered German defenses determined to sell their skins dearly in the sector of Tailleville and the radar camp at Douvres-la-Délivrande. Although they managed to link up with the British from Gold Beach at Creully, the 3rd Canadian Division failed either to wrest highway 13 or Carpiquet from the enemy. The front line positions reached on the evening of D-Day would remain practically unchanged for over a month.

Sword

It was the 3rd British Division (General Rennie) that had been allocated the task of capturing the town of Caen, on the evening of D-Day, at the same time linking up with the 6th Airborne Division that had been dropped on the east bank of the Orne, and with the 3rd Canadian Division that had landed to its right. After the liberation of Ouistreham, carried out with the help of the Franco-British Kieffer commando, the division encountered stout resistance in front of the high ground at Périers-sur-le-Dan (on the Hillman site). The time lost in reducing this niche, containing around twenty fortified structures, was sufficient for the Germans to take up a solid defensive position to the north of Caen and enabled them to block the advance of the British towards the capital of Lower Normandy for more than a month.

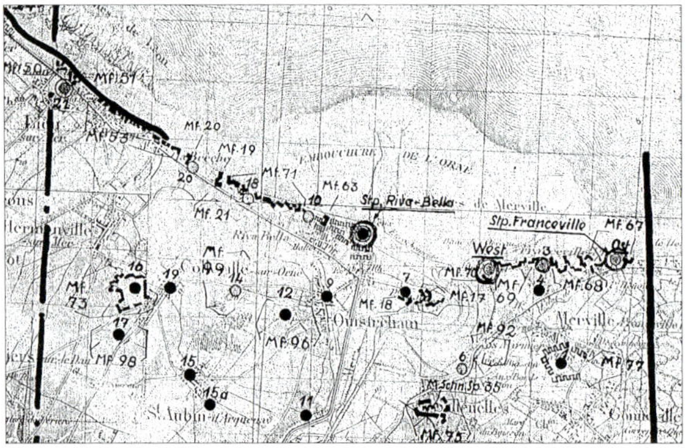

German map showing the defenses in the Orne Bay. We can see the Merville artillery position, the coastal defenses at Franceville, the base of operations at Riva Bella and, inland, the field general's command post.

THE KIEFFER COMMANDO IN OUISTREHAM

"Suddenly, through a gap in the smoke, the underwater defenses, stakes and "hedgehogs" entangled with barbed wire, loomed up before us. We had arrived. [...] The big question was: "Were we in front of our landing point?" Yes we were. The demolished walls of the children's holiday camp where we were supposed to muster were straight in front of us."

Commandant Kieffer

Lanternier, a marine belonging to the Kieffer commando, on the evening of June 6 in Amfreville.

Aerial view of the assault on Sword Beach (Hermanville breach sector).

THE INVASION ANNOUNCED ON CANADIAN RADIO

"At 3.30 this morning, the government was officially informed that the invasion of western Europe had begun. [...] May all Canadians offer up a silent prayer today for the success of our forces and those of our Allies, and for the liberation of Europe."

Mackenzie King, Canadian Prime Minister

Gathering of men from the 3rd British Infantry Division in the sector of Sword Beach.

The response of the Militärmaschinerie of the west front

The overall response to the Allied assault was fierce but the strength of this resistance would vary from service to service. Without ever endangering the Allied operation, the forces of the *Kriegsmarine* in the Channel turned out to be extremely aggressive. Although they only had a smattering of small units, half of which were based at Le Havre, where the occupying forces had built a large concrete shelter, the German navy was in action every night against the concentrations of ships of the Allied fleet *"an der Nordküste der Normandie zwischen Le Havre und Cherbourg"* [on the north coast of Normandy between Le Havre and Cherbourg]. With the help of torpedoes, the *Schnell-Boote* (high-speed patrol boats) managed to sink several units and create confusion among the landing fleet. In order to put a

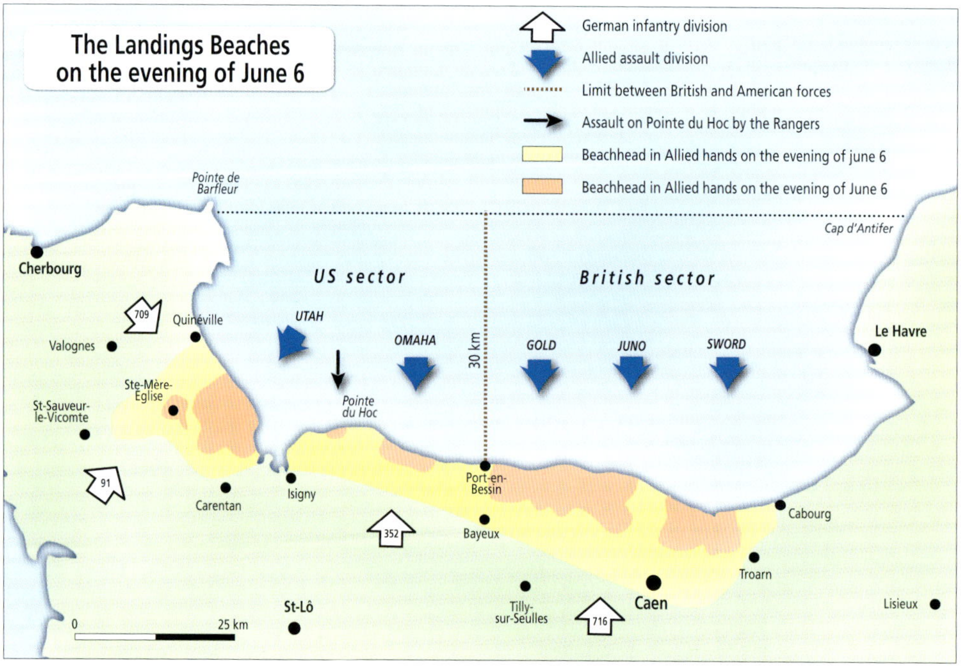

Any landing must be accompanied by control in the air. Douglas A20 in observation above the beachhead.

Identification of those killed on the beach.

stop to the comings and goings of these patrol boats, the air force proceeded to bomb the naval base at Le Havre on June 14. This air raid, which destroyed or damaged around fifty ships, and another to follow at the Boulogne base, sounded the death knell for the activities of the *Kriegsmarine* in the Channel. During these two air raids, the strategic air force used what were known as earthquake bombs, weighing 6 tons, which were launched from a height of 20,000 feet for maximum effect. This new bomb had been tested a few days earlier, on June 8, on the Saumur rail tunnel, to prevent reinforcements from the south of France reaching the Normandy front by train at night.

Since the beginning of 1944, the 3rd *Luftflotte* (3rd air fleet) had been incapable of commanding the air space in the west, and when the invasion came, it was to put up a much poorer showing than had been anticipated. According to Allied reports on D-Day, less than a hundred German fighters flew over the assault sector, ten to twenty times fewer than what Allied military experts had forecast! The first appearance of a swastika over the beaches was not until Tuesday June 6, at around 3 p.m., i.e. about 9 hours after the start of the seaborne assault and 15 hours after the first paratroops had landed! As it turned out, the fiercest resistance came on land, from the shore-based divisions (709th, 352th and 716th), the 91st Division of the *Luftwaffe*, the 6th Paratroop Regiment, and lastly from the tank units (21st Division, *Panzerlehr* and 12th SS Armored). The latter unit had undergone intensive training and was raring to take up the challenge. They had been waiting for the big showdown with the Allies for weeks, and were determined to prove their superiority and give the Anglo-Americans a hiding. Up against soldiers like this, who had no intention of giving an inch of ground, preferring to fight without mercy to the last man, the Allies would pay a high price for final victory.

THE GERMANS DISCOVER THE AMERICAN PLANS

Generals Rommel (on the right) and Speidel, chief-of-staff of Army Group B (headquarters La Roche-Guyon).

Too good to be true, this could be the title of the story that follows. In the evening of June 6, Caucasian soldiers who had been incorporated into the German 352nd Infantry Division discovered the body of an American officer and a briefcase containing various documents in the mouth of the Vire. Among these papers, there was a plan of operations for 7th US Army Corps, a formation whose brief was to cut the Cotentin in two and capture Cherbourg! It was an extraordinary find. Forty-eight hours after the start of the cross-Channel invasion, the defenders had under their very eyes the plans indicating the Americans' scheduled movements in Normandy!

From 352nd Division's intelligence officer, the documents were passed on up the normal channels till they reached Saint-Lô and the headquarters of 84th Army Corps under General Marcks, then to Le Mans and the offices of 7th Army. At this point Pemsel, Dollmann's chief of staff, made a detailed analysis of the documents and passed on a summary that reached Rommel's headquarters at La Roche-Guyon early in the morning of June 8, and on again to Saint-Germain-en-Laye (Marshal von Rundstedt). From there, the news reached the Chancellery in Berlin.

According to General Pemsel, the scale of the operations envisaged by the Americans in their documents (the capture of Cherbourg, then the invasion of Brittany) required so many troops that these operations automatically ruled out any second landing in the north of France. In spite of this clear-sighted analysis, Hitler continued to hold the opposite view. Full of mistrust, the German dictator could not help considering his troops' discovery as a ploy and a stratagem of the Allied secret service. Nothing could change this deep conviction: in Hitler's opinion, there were still several dozen Allied divisions in England waiting to cross the Pas-de-Calais. A second landing was imminent and this time he would not be taken by surprise.

The situation on the evening of D-Day

On the evening of D-Day, the Allies had managed to obtain a foothold on the continent. More than 150,000 soldiers had been landed by air and sea, together with approximately 20,000 vehicles of all types. On the whole, Overlord was a success and Eisenhower could be satisfied with what had been accomplished on the ground with a great deal of determination and suffering by courageous men.

"Heavy though they were, casualties incurred on D-Day were far smaller than had been expected." By the end of the day, out of the 155,000 men at the beachhead (75,000 British, 57,000 Americans and 23,000 paras), the losses (killed, wounded or missing) totaled 10,000 soldiers (3,000 for the British, 6,000 for the Americans and 1,300 for the paras), or seven per cent of the numbers engaged.

The British press on the evening of June 6, in London.

A journalist recording his report. Press correspondents could sometimes use the broadcasting services of the British army for live reports on the BBC.

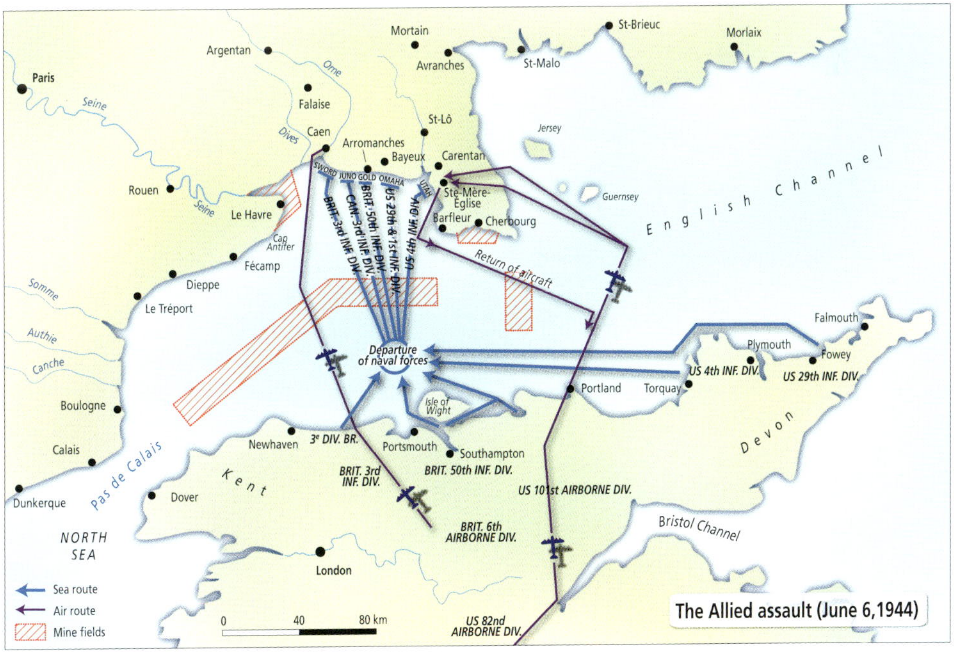

British prisoner.

IN BERLIN…

In Berlin, well aware that the invasion would determine the outcome of the war, Hitler wrote an "Aufruf an die Soldaten im Westen" [appeal to the soldiers on the western front] a few days after the Allied assault. In this solemn proclamation, the Führer called on his soldiers to fight bitterly, to hold out or die, because everyone knew "dass niemals kapituliert wird" [that there would never be a surrender].

KTB [war diary] Nr. 5 of the 15th Army

The total killed on June 6 lies somewhere between two and three per cent.

Admittedly, the objectives set for the evening of June 6 were not all attained, but there was no question of feeling demoralized or throwing in the towel. This was not the spring of 1940! Now that the beachhead had been secured, it had to be consolidated prior to breaking out. To paraphrase the speech made by Churchill at Mansion House in London on November 10, 1942, the day after the British victory at El Alamein in Egypt, the Allied leaders could observe on the evening of June 6 that the Normandy invasion maybe did not put an end to the war but at least the success of this operation meant that, from now on, the end of the beginning was well behind them and the beginning of the end could not be too far off! Without a shadow of doubt, one of the most momentous achievements in 20th century world history had just taken place in Normandy.

Variety and power of the military equipment on the beaches from the very first evening.

IN LONDON...

"All day, it was difficult to imagine, while London was quietly going about its business, that, not far away, fierce fighting was taking place on the French coast."

A. Brooke, British Chief of the Imperial General Staff

Medical Battalion from the 4th US Infantry Division tends to a soldier with a leg injury.

THE BATTLE OF NORMANDY

JUNE 7-AUGUST 21, 1944

We may consider the long battle of Normandy (June 7-August 21, 1944) in three main stages, each roughly coinciding with a month of the summer of 1944. June was devoted to cutting off the Cotentin peninsula and to the American conquest of the *Festung* (fortress) of Cherbourg. After a long period of slow progress both in the bocage and in the plain, on the opposite flank, July brought three pieces of good news: the capture of Saint-Lô, the liberation of Caen, and the collapse of the front and break-out towards Avranches. The month of August was filled with murderous fighting and after almost 80 days of struggle saw the end of the battle with the encircling of the 7th German Army in the Falaise Gap.

MONTGOMERY'S STRATEGY

"Once we had secured a good footing in Normandy, my plan was to threaten to break out on the eastern flank, that is in the Caen sector. By pursuing this threat I intended to draw the main enemy reserves, particularly his armored divisions into that sector and to keep them there – using the British and Canadian forces for this purpose."

B. L. Montgomery

Opposite: A typical Normandy farmer and an American soldier belonging to the Civil Affairs service.

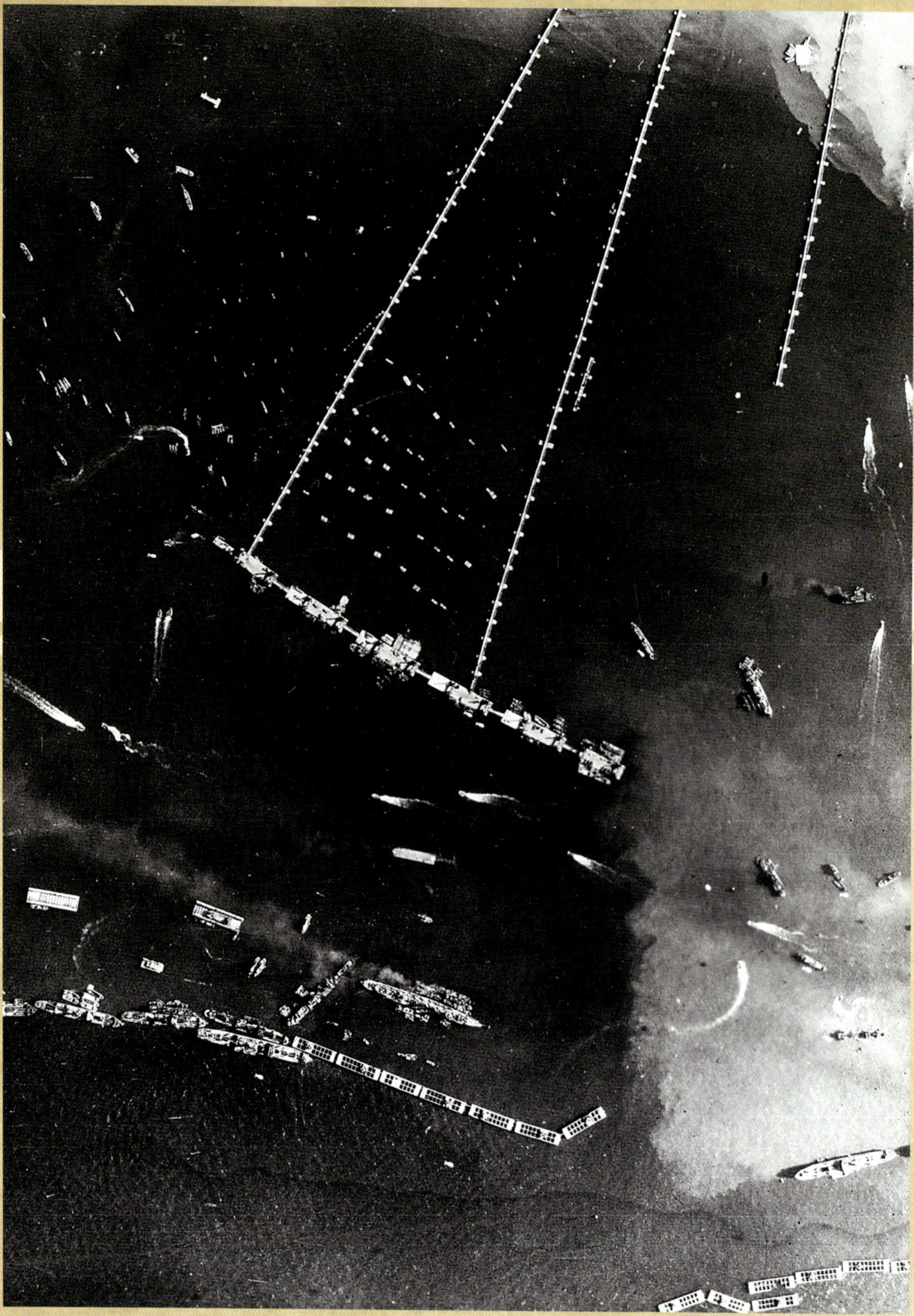

A superb aerial view of the artificial harbor at Arromanches. We can see from the top of the photo going downwards, the floating causeways, the quays on piles and the breakwater made of old ships and concrete caissons.

JUNE 1944: THE CAPTURE OF A PORT

"We knew that even after we captured Cherbourg its port capacity could not meet all our needs. To solve this problem we undertook a project so unique as to be classed by many scoffers as completely fantastic. It was a plan to construct artificial harbors on the coast of Normandy."

D. D. Eisenhower, Crusade in Europe

The Allied plan

By the evening of D-Day, the Allies had secured a foothold on the continent. The brutal and bloody throwing back into the sea promised by German propaganda had failed to materialize. This was a far cry from the muddle of Jubilee! "Overlord was in the bag". That was at least true for the phase of the plan involving the troop landings. Otherwise, the job was as yet far from finished: beachheads had to be consolidated, airfields captured or set up, mulberries had to be assembled, continental ports captured, fuel supplies ensured, reinforcements brought in, wounded and prisoners evacuated and, most of all, German counter-attacks by sea, land or air, expected on D+3 or D+4, had to be repulsed.

Marshals von Rundstedt and Rommel, with General Zimmermann in the background, in Saint Germain-en-Laye. Rommel was deeply disappointed at *Führer*'s refusal to give him full authority over the armored divisions stationed on the western front.

The battle plan for the Normandy campaign was a textbook affair drawn up by Montgomery, who had been appointed to command the American and British land armed forces for Overlord. The British forces, placed in the eastern sector of the beachhead, were given the task of drawing the German tank divisions. With this aim in mind, on the day after D-Day, Montgomery's troops were to spearhead a thrust towards Caen giving the enemy to believe that the Allies' prime objective was to cross the Orne, head off towards Paris and on to Germany itself. To keep up relentless pressure on the enemy and tie him down with the constant threat of breaking out, in such a way as to force him to commit the main part of his fighting reserves around the capital of Lower Normandy, this was the task assigned to the British. By giving the Germans such a bone to chew on in the Caen sector, Montgomery made progress in the Cotentin easier for the Americans. On the mobile wing of the Allied armies, the Americans under Bradley were to cut off the peninsula, capture Cherbourg, break out southwards and finally move up northwards to meet the British in order to encircle 7th German Army in a wide pocket.

Based on the principle of keeping the German forces divided, Montgomery's plan was that when one of the Allies launched an offensive, the other, who was located at the opposite side of the front, would launch an operation at the same time, so as to avoid a transfer of the enemy troops from one wing to another. So when the Americans broke out towards Cherbourg (June 18-26), the

British launched Operation Epsom, south of Caen. Later, to relieve the Americans during their offensive on Saint-Lô, Monty launched Operation Charnwood (the liberation of Caen) in his sector. In a final example of this strategy, to help the US break-out in the Cotentin (Operation Cobra, July 25), the British tried to pin down the German armored divisions between Caen and Falaise by launching the Goodwood and Spring offensives (July 18-25). There were a few problems of synchronization, in particular during Operation Epsom, whose launch was delayed by the great storm. But apart from the gale that disrupted the landing of troops for this offensive, the operations on the Normandy front were successfully coordinated during the summer of 1944. In this strategic plan, the British, whose mission was to immobilize as many *Panzer* divisions as possible around Caen, would only be able to gain ground very gradually with small operations in June and July, as the German defense was solid and deep. On the other side of the front, however, where there were three times fewer *Panzers*, the Americans could maneuver more easily. This meant that the war communiqués give the impression that Bradley's soldiers were much more willing to fight than the Tommies. In practice, this was not at all the case, and it should be remembered that the fabulous cavalcade of the US Army in the south of the Cotentin which began on July 25 was only possible thanks to the relentless efforts and persistence of the British around Caen. As for Rommel, by favoring the defense of his right wing, he would fall in the trap prepared for him by the victor of El Alamein. As Eddy Bauer, the Swiss war specialist, wrote: in Normandy, Rommel would dance to Montgomery's music!

In the Allied camp, the war was led by Montgomery and Bradley.

Consolidation of the beachhead

On the evening of June 6, the Anglo-Americans had not achieved all their objectives and only two British beaches (Gold and Juno) had been joined up. The first task of the troops was thus to link up the different beachheads in order to prevent the Germans counter-attacking down the corridors separating the assault beaches, as they had tried to do between Sword and Juno, and, through their skill and the superiority of their tanks, picking off the Allied forces one by one.

Ardenne Abbey in the 1950s. In the days following the assault on the beaches, a regiment of grenadiers from the *12. SS. Pz. Division*, who had arrived as reinforcements to the west of Caen, overstepped the law of war and assassinated over a hundred Canadian prisoners at various places on the front, in particular in the enclosure of Ardenne Abbey. Kurt Meyer, the commander of this regiment, would be judged at the end of the war by a Canadian military tribunal, condemned to death but not executed, and finally liberated in 1954.

BAYEUX

"I have just travelled about twenty miles across the liberated sector of France before coming to the main street in Bayeux. The whole town has put out flags. The townspeople are showering flowers on our soldiers, but they are now paying special attention to the traitors who collaborated with Germany. [...] This is how the people of France [...] are letting off steam. They do so by showing how glad they are to see us, and especially by giving a free rein to four years of suppressed hatred, hatred of the Germans and their accomplices."

A British journalist

British soldiers near Bayeux cathedral. *"We have lost Bayeux, which is not particularly important, but it might nevertheless be a bad omen."* (Goebbels, *Diaries*, June 1944.)

On June 7, the British troops who had landed on Gold Beach entered Bayeux and continued to advance inland, whilst trying to make contact with the Americans who had landed at Omaha. On the way, three miles west of Arromanches, they captured the garrison of the Longues-sur-Mer shore battery in the early hours without a shot being fired. For their part, the Americans of Omaha, whilst seeking to make contact with the troops that came ashore to their right at Utah, sent out reconnaissance parties in the direction of Port-en-Bessin in order to link up with the British. This was achieved a few hours after the capture of Port-en-Bessin by the 47th Commando of the Royal Marines. Thus, by June 8, the Allies held a continuous forty-mile-long strip of shore along the Calvados

General de Gaulle in Bayeux, June 14.

coastline extending from the Orne estuary to the Vire estuary. With Courseulles taken almost intact by the Canadians, Montgomery had two ports to unload supplies for the Allied Expeditionary Force. In the first of a series of visits, Churchill landed at Courseulles on June 12, and two days later, it was General de Gaulle's turn to set foot on French soil and make a speech in Bayeux in which he confirmed the authority of the Provisional Government of the Republic. On June 12, D+6, the Americans of Omaha crossed the river Vire and established contact with troops under General Collins who had come ashore at Utah. With this further link-up, the beachhead was now fifty miles long and the front was about twelve miles deep, with the deepest

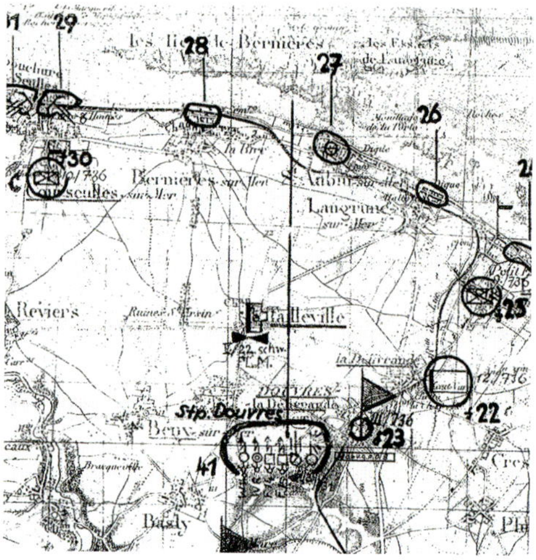

Map from the archives of the 716th division which mentions the *Luftwaffe* radar station in Douvres. Located around 6 miles north of Caen and spread over around 25 acres, the radar station had around 30 bunkers. At the center of this large camp, five radar antennae permanently monitored the sky and sea above the Channel. The Douvres *Festung* would put up fierce resistance to the assaults by the Allied troops until June 17.

Liberation of Carentan, June 12.

penetration towards Saint-Lô and Caumont. That same day, after fierce fighting against the soldiers of General von der Heydte's 6th Parachute Regiment, the Americans captured Carentan and also the heavy artillery battery at Saint Marcouf-Crisbecq. With these exploits behind them, they headed off towards Barneville, a small seaside town on the west coast of the Cotentin, straight across from Utah, that had been reached on June 18. Having thus cut off the northern sector of the peninsula, Bradley ordered Collins to start moving up towards Cherbourg. The previous day at Margival near Soissons, von Rundstedt and Rommel had had a stormy meeting with Hitler about the situation in Normandy.

After a hard-fought battle, Montebourg fell on June 19, then Valognes, in ruins, two days later. Cherbourg was now only twelve miles away. It was at this moment that the US forces laid hands on several dozen secret weapon (V1 and V2) launching sites.

The despair of those who have lost everything as a result of the fighting and bombardments.

Valognes after the American bombardments.

Refugees on the road on the outskirts of Valognes.

VALOGNES

"The houses are suddenly disappearing and all that remains is a heap of stones. This is not merely destroyed houses, this is total collapse. Nothing has resisted the bombs. Nothing remains standing..."

Jacques Kayser, A journalist on the Normandy front

Artificial harbors: a challenge to technology

In order to ensure supplies reached the expeditionary forces until such time as the harbor installations at Cherbourg were captured, the Allied planners had banked on setting up two artificial harbors, one off the American sector, and the other off the British sector. Considered to be a deciding factor in the success of the operation in the Bay of the Seine, this bold innovation had received the blessing of the top military authorities at the Quebec conference. The basic idea of prefabricated harbors was straightforward enough, involving the creation of a double area of water sheltered from the swell off the Calvados coast by constructing two artificial breakwaters. Within this sheltered water, unloading facilities would be provided with platforms linked by piers to dry land. Built in sections in Great Britain, the entire installation was to be towed across the Channel by

General view of the installations at Arromanches artificial harbor (early August 1944). The photo shows, from left to right: the artificial breakwater made of old boats, extended and strengthened by large concrete caissons (Phoenixes), the 1,200 acre artificial anchorage, the line of quays on piles and the floating causeways. Passes enabled traffic to enter and exit the harbor. In August, in one day, 18,836 vehicles would pass through the quays of the artificial harbor, the equivalent to 785 an hour or one every 4 seconds!

Located in front of the artificial harbors, around 2,200 yards from the shore, the first breakwater made of a row of floating rafts known as bombardons constituted the long-range defense of the harbor against the swell. The bombardons were made of hollow metal caissons in the shape of a cross.

tugs, the day after D-Day. According to the scheme, each mulberry (code name for the artificial harbors) was to be capable of handling 7,000 tons of stores and 1,250 vehicles per day, from D+15 (June 21) onwards, and was to remain in service until the beginning of the fall of 1944. At that time, it was thought that there would be a sufficient volume of maritime traffic going through whatever continental ports had by then been taken to make the mulberries redundant.

The first task was to find a solution to the three most awkward problems: creating sheltered anchorages, building quays for unloading purposes, and finally, linking the quays to the land. In answer to the first question as to how to set apart an area of calm water, it was decided to sink a line of old blockships, extended by concrete blocks or caissons (known as Phoenixes), around the coast, about 3/4 mile out. Behind this sea wall, small landing craft and medium-sized cargo ships could readily be accommodated. For the biggest ships with drafts requiring deeper waters to anchor in, it was decided to add an outer anti-swell barrier, made up of elements of a new type called "bombardons", towards the open sea in front of the Phoenixes.

A Phoenix caisson under construction.

On the caissons, anti-aircraft defense equipment protected the artificial harbor.

Below: On June 7, in the morning, a breakwater made of old boats weighed down with concrete (known as blockships) was installed behind the bombardons. This sea wall was given the code name "gooseberry".

Inside the first sheltered anchorage, the one enclosed by concrete caissons, unloading quays or pierheads were to be installed. These were platforms of over two acres in area capable of following the movements of the tide by sliding up and down long piles resting on the sea bed. This ingenious system prevented unloading operations being interrupted at any time. The most delicate question to be settled was linking the wharves to dry land, because of the instability of the sea surface. After many tests, a system of relatively flexible metal roadways resting on steel caissons was adopted.

Interesting aerial photograph taken on June 15, before the storm, by the US Air Force. In the center of the shot is the beach known as Dog Red (Les Moulins, a hamlet in Saint-Laurent-sur-Mer). To the right of Les Moulins, the beach continues in the direction of Colleville (Easy Green); to the far left, the village of Vierville. From top to bottom, the aerial photograph shows the barrage of bombardons positioned in a single line and some high-draft ships at anchor, the breakwater made of lines of Phoenix caissons, a large entrance pass, then the breakwater created by the blockships divided into several sections, on the right the zigzag line of a long anti-tank ditch blocking the entrance to the wooded Ruquet valley, and the construction of an advanced landing ground at the top of the plateau between Les Moulins and Ruquet valley.

Setting up the two artificial harbors

According to the initial schedule, the artificial harbors were due to be completed by the end of June. At Omaha, where things were going well, a row of bombardons, fifteen blockships for the gooseberry, thirty or so Phoenixes, a landing pier for LSTs (Landing Ship Tanks) and two quays on piles were up and running by June 17. On June 18, 11,000 men, 2,000 vehicles and 9,000 tons of supplies were brought ashore via the American mulberry. In the British sector too, in spite of the difficulties caused by the wind and tidal

Set in the center of the artificial anchorage created by the blockships and caissons, the platforms used as quays could follow the movements of the tide by sliding along four piles. This system meant that supplies could be unloaded regardless of the tide.

currents, they had their work cut out installing the enormous concrete blocks that the tugs had to hold in place for the nearly half an hour it took to fill them. The day before the equinoctial storm, several piers and two quays on piles were already in place in the vast anchorage opposite Arromanches. In addition to the traffic passing through the two artificial harbors, there were also direct unloading operations on the beaches as well as those carried out in the smaller ports of Lower Normandy (Courseulles and Port-en-Bessin, open to coasters from June 12). By June 18 (D+12) there were on the continent, in the territorial base held along the Channel, a total of approximately 600,000 men, 100,000 vehicles and a week's rations and ammunition in advance. Petrol supplies were made by directly unloading it in jerrycans on the harbor quays, on the beaches or through flexible semi-underwater hoses which connected tankers at anchor out to sea with storage tanks installed at Port-en-Bessin and Sainte-Honorine-des-Pertes where the fuel was stocked. In short, the day before the June 19 gale, the situation was by no means catastrophic: the landings kept a steady two days behind schedule. With the forthcoming opening of the two artificial harbors, there was reason to hope that something could be done to remove what backlog there was. However, the storm temporarily put paid to such fine optimism.

The great storm (June 19-22, 1944)

On June 19, the barometer suddenly dropped steeply and an unforecast gale blew up from nowhere, whilst ominously high waves began to appear in the sea. The storm was to rage for the next seventy-two hours with occasional gusts of over 45 mph. In the gusts, the rows of bombardons began to drift. These huge metal cases went berserk, causing tremendous injury to the Phoenixes. In the violence of the waves passing over the blockships, the quays on piles were shaken and even overturned at Omaha Beach.

On the morning of June 22, after three days of hell, the damage to the artificial harbors was enormous: bombardons completely destroyed, blockships displaced, numerous caissons smashed and eight hundred craft run aground in a great pile-up on the beaches. It was at Omaha, where the artificial harbor was by now in indescribable chaos, that the situation was the most catastrophic. The Allies had lost more material through bad weather in the space of just three days than since the start of D-Day from attacks by the Germans. They hoped that the capture of the port of Cherbourg would help them to make up the backlog in unloading.

Photo showing the great storm in the Channel in June 1944.

Linking the unloading quays to dry land, the piers were positioned at regular intervals on floats. Telescopic spans absorbed deformation and torsion to the structure caused by the movement of the waves. Cargo ships were mostly unloaded on the quays or directly into amphibious trucks (DUKWs) which went back and forth between the ships and the depots located behind the beaches.

The secret German weapons in the Cotentin

Being relatively close to the southern coast of Britain (Portsmouth is only 90 miles from Cherbourg), in 1944 the Cotentin peninsula was crammed with German military installations. In addition to the radar and radio navigation stations in The Hague and the Val de Saire, south of Cherbourg, there were many densely packed secret weapon (V1 and V2) launching sites. These mystery installations were captured by troops under General Collins, on their way up to Cherbourg.

The V1 was a small plane, simple and cheap to manufacture in the underground factories of the *Reich*; it was 25 feet long with

Aerial view of the north-west part of the Cotentin peninsula: the foreground shows Vauville cove; in the far west is the peninsula of La Hague and the Nez de Jobourg; in the north, at the center of the coast, is Cherbourg harbor.

an 18 foot wingspan and weighed roughly 2 tons including its 2000 lb warhead. The propulsion mechanism placed over the fuselage comprised an 11'6" long exhaust pipe containing a jet engine. Flying at speeds of approximately 375 mph and altitudes from 2000 to 2800 feet, the V1 was aimed directly at a town in southern England, launched from a ramp, reaching its target after a flight lasting about twenty minutes.

The V1 was launched by means of the catapult procedure already in use on aircraft carriers. In the first installations at least, both ramp and catapult were protected by two concrete walls, as can be seen in the photograph opposite. Apart from the ramp, a V1 launching station comprised roughly ten other buildings (galleries serving as stores for the plane, an assembly area, concrete shelters for storing the chemicals required to operate the catapult, explosive stores, fine-tuning workshop, ranging station...). Not a single V1 was fired from the Cherbourg peninsula. The first was launched from ramps sited in the north of France during the night of June 12 to 13 a week after the invasion.

V1 launch ramp, partially destroyed by the enemy before its retreat (north of France). On this second-generation ramp, the protective side walls have been removed.

American soldiers on the site of the first-generation ramp in Brix (or Sottevast for the Allies). In his journal, Galtier-Boissière compared the new German weapons *"to the* Gross Bertha *of 1918, only more malicious"*.

V2 rocket on the launching pad. According to Goebbels, who witnessed a launch, the noise at the moment of the launch was horrendous: *"[...] the ground shakes and it feels like the end of the world."* Propaganda claimed that the *neue Waffen* (new weapons) would lead to a reversal of the situation in the favor of the *Reich*.

The V2 rocket was a revolutionary device 15 yards high and weighed 13 tons at take-off including 9 tons of fuel and oxidant. The fuel used was methanol (5,070 lb) and 14,770 lb of liquid oxygen provided the oxidant required to work the missile's engine insofar as its flight path took it for most of the time into empty space beyond the upper layers of the atmosphere. Each rocket carried a ton of explosive placed in the nose of the missile. In order to escape the pull of gravity, the rocket engine, which got up to 700,000 HP, was powered by a mighty turbopump. With an entirely new, innovative model of immense technical achievement, the turbopump was capable of discharging nearly

450 lb of fuel per second into the combustion chamber! A long-range rocket designed for bombing Britain's large cities, the V2 was the first ballistic missile in history and the ancestor of all modern rockets, whether Saturn or Soyuz. Under the action of its propellant the V2 had an absolutely vertical take-off position. There was no question of any ramp. Propulsion was ensured through the extremely high expulsion rate of the liquids contained in the tanks. With an initial thrust of 25 tons, it reached the speed of sound in less than half a minute. At an altitude of 30 miles, and still climbing, the rocket began to level out in the programmed direction. A minute after blast-off, 30 miles up, when the missile was flying through the stratosphere, its speed was close to 3,750 mph, five times the speed of sound. After a ground station cut off fuel combustion, the missile carried on its upward movement, then fell down onto its objective at a speed of 2,200 mph. The entire flight lasted under 300 seconds. After burying itself several yards into the ground, due to the effect of its speed, the diabolical missile would explode, producing a crater about forty yards in diameter.

Owing to the number and complexity of the operations to be carried out before launching, the German high command had built special bunkers in northern France and in the Cherbourg peninsula. In the Cotentin, a giant bunker was constructed in the village of Brix, south of Cherbourg. Designed to house a hundred missiles as well as the chemicals required for launching, this vast installation was never completed following Allied bombing raids. The first V2 rocket fired against London was launched from Holland, on September 8, 1944, not from a bunker but from a simple concrete slab!

Giant bunker in Brix, at the end of June 1944, as the American troops arrived.

The capture of the Festung (fortress) of Cherbourg

Faced with fierce resistance from certain fortified positions and General von Schlieben's refusal to surrender, General Collins requested the help of the US Navy in order to neutralize the *Marineküstenbatterien* (the marine coastal batteries: York, Brommy, Hamburg...) installed along the northern coast of the Cotentin. Following this appeal for help, a naval fleet was assembled in Portland, not far from Weymouth, and placed under the command of Admiral Deyo.

Marauder returning from a bombing mission on the coastal defenses at Cherbourg.

Opposite: **US generals Bradley and Collins in the Cotentin.**
"In Caen, we were keeping the Germans on our left, while we were dealing them a blow from the right in the direction of Cherbourg."
(Eisenhower, *Crusade in Europe*.)

Divided into two groups, the fleet detailed to bombard the German defenses at Cherbourg and the surrounding area included five heavy American battleships (the *Tuscaloosa*, *Texas*, *Arkansas*, *Quincy* and *Nevada*) and two British battleships (the *Glasgow* and the *Enterprise*). This group was accompanied by a dozen destroyers, a flotilla of mine-sweepers and air cover. Beginning at noon or thereabouts, on Sunday June 25, the

Aerial view of Cherbourg harbor taken by the US Air Force.

240-mm caliber gun from the Fermanville coastal battery known as Hamburg. The casemate had not yet been given its roof.

fighting would last roughly 3 hours. After the York battery (Querqueville) had opened fire with its 4170-mm guns placed in casemates, hitting the *Glasgow* but without causing any serious damage, the US battleship *Nevada* tried to silence the German position, with supporting fire from the *Tuscaloosa* and the *Quincy*. Using its large modern 355-mm caliber guns with a range of 44,000 yards, the *Nevada* scored one direct hit without silencing the three other German pieces. In its turn, the *Glasgow* joined in the fun and tried to neutralize the battery of four 150-mm guns installed at Castel-Vendon, about eight miles

US Navy battleship *Nevada* off the coast of Cherbourg on June 25, 1944. On the morning of June 6, the mission of the *Nevada*, a survivor from Pearl Harbor with huge 14-inch caliber pieces of artillery, was to neutralize the Crisbecq (Saint-Marcouf) German coastal battery, constructed just behind Utah assault beach.

west of Cherbourg. Meanwhile, the destroyers were busy knocking out various strongholds along the shore whose position had been indicated to them by General Collins, himself observing the naval battle from the hills to the south of the town (works at the Fort de l'Est, the Jetée des Flamands, the Arsenal...).

Whilst group 1, placed under the command of Admiral Deyo, was engaged in destroying the defenses situated west of the port of Cherbourg, group 2 (Admiral Bryant, US Navy) had been detailed to silence the Brommy (Tourlaville) and Hamburg (Fermanville) batteries. If Brommy was the twin sister of Castel-Vendon, Hamburg, on the other hand, with its four 240-mm fixed guns with a range of twenty-five miles, was the largest artillery emplacement in the whole Bay of the Seine. In the absence of the Nevada which had still not had it out with York, the task fell to the Arkansas, a battleship built before the First World War, and the Texas of silencing the Hamburg's guns, placed in emplacements that were still unfinished in June 1944. Using their old 14-inch (355-mm) and 12-inch (305-mm) guns with a range of a dozen or so miles, the Texas and the Arkansas showered the artillery positions at Fermanville, totally destroying a gun. In the midst of the action, a gale whipped up, blowing away the smoke-screen that was concealing the revered battleships. Immediately taking advantage of the situation, a large German gun was aimed straight at the target, causing significant damage to the Texas. In total, at around 3 p.m., by the time Admiral Deyo gave the signal for the return to Portland, the Texas, which 19 days earlier had showered the Pointe du Hoc, had fired 206 355-mm shells on Hamburg, the Arkansas 58 305-mm shells and the 5 escorting destroyers 552 127-mm shots.

Periscope in a command bunker in the sector of Cherbourg.

Although it did not completely silence the German coastal batteries, the naval bombardment, combined with the aerial bombardment and violent artillery fire from the army, according to Admiral Krancke and General Schlieben had a disastrous effect on the morale of the Cherbourg garrison. Coming in behind this deluge of steel, the American troops entered the town on the following day and in the afternoon of June 26 obtained the unconditional surrender of von Schlieben and Admiral Hennecke at around 3 p.m.

THE SURRENDER OF GENERAL VON SCHLIEBEN

On learning that General Karl von Schlieben, commander of the Festung Cherbourg (Fortress Cherbourg), had just repeated Marshal von Paulus's gesture of capitulation in Stalingrad, Hitler was boiling with rage:
"It must be ensured that the most valiant officers are placed in command of the fortresses and not such braggarts as the type that we had at Cherbourg..."
Speaking of this gang of high-ranking officers, he added: "They are nothing but cowards who have been educated in such a way that they consider it perfectly natural [...] for others to make sacrifices whilst they themselves refuse to get stuck in. [...] This is intolerable [...] We are behaving like the Italians in acclaiming these miserable and spineless cowards as if they were heroes."
Helmut Heiber (presented by), Hitler parle à ses généraux, Albin Michel, 1964

Cherbourg. Underground passage in the headquarters of General von Schlieben, commander of the *Festung* of Cherbourg. *"The loss of Cherbourg represents a considerable failure."* (Goebbels, *Diaries*, June 29, 1944.)

General von Schlieben and Admiral Hennecke at the headquarters of General Collins in the Château de Servigny, in the town of Yvetot-Bocage, near Valognes.

In total, by the end of June, the Americans had lost almost 20,000 men, but they had finally seized the installations of a big continental port even though more than a week behind schedule. The trouble was that the US Navy had been prepared to find the port in a semi-demolished state, but what met their eyes was far worse than their worst fears: dynamited wharves, road beds cluttered with blockhouses or broken up, railway lines ripped out, unusable docks cluttered with wrecks, railway terminal and sheds in ruins, cranes thrown down at the foot of the wharves, mines and all kinds of traps placed in the mud of the docks or under rolls of barbed wire to prevent them being defused... It was an utter disaster and an apocalyptic sight. It took a considerable amount of time to clear the docks, to refloat over a hundred wrecks, repair the breaches in the quays, complete mine-sweeping operations, re-establish the roadways and

THE FRENCH TRY THEIR TRAITORS

"The natives of Normandy are a conservative, orderly people. When the Germans were driven out of the Norman towns by the Allies, the Frenchmen showed none of the violence against collaborationists which the rest of the world expected. Even when dealing with out-and-out traitors, the Normans kept within the law. In the first trial of collaborationists to take place on French soil since the beginning of the invasion, a Cherbourg military tribunal tried and convicted two miserable young Frenchmen who had spied on Allied troops for the Germans. Instead of being executed, the two spies were sentenced to life imprisonment."

***Life*, July 1944**

Cherbourg. Arresting traitors.

Column of German prisoners of war in Cherbourg, June 1944.

railways and reconstruct the working tools (lifting and handling equipment...). Shortly before the end of July, the first liberty-ship entered the sheltered water of the large port in the Cotentin: its cargo was not unloaded on the quays but on Napoleon beach by a fleet of amphibious trucks. Whatever could not be unloaded at Cherbourg was therefore directly unloaded on Omaha beach from the large LSTs. Only in the second half of September would the "port of freedom" start to operate at full capacity, but by this time the Battle of Normandy had been over for more than three weeks. The capture of the harbor installations in Cherbourg marked the end of the amphibious phase of Overlord. With a solid rear base, the Allied operation in the Bay of the Seine became an ordinary military campaign, freeing up the majority of the naval forces that had been gathered for the Normandy operation. The large US warships left the Channel to strengthen the Task Forces in the Pacific in the operation to capture the Mariana Islands.

Epsom or the battle of the Odon

(June 25-30)

Whilst the Americans were fighting a difficult battle in order to enter Cherbourg, at the other end of the front, following their failed attempt at capturing Villers-Bocage in mid-June, the British were preparing to launch a new offensive. Code-named Epsom, the objective of this powerful attack spearheaded by 60,000 men with 400 armored vehicles in support was to capture Caen and its airfield. In reality, without air support due to bad weather, the encircling movement around Caen from the west was quickly contained by the *Panzer* divisions and the airfield at Carpiquet which the RAF wanted so badly stayed out of reach. If Epsom was a fiasco, the *Gegenangriff* (counter-attack) launched in

British tanks destroyed at the entrance to Villers-Bocage on June 13, after the failure of Montgomery's attempt to surround Caen from the south.

Piper from the 15th Scotland Division on the way to the front, located on the left bank of the Odon.

the Caen sector by the former *Panzergruppe West*, since renamed *5. Panzerarmee* (5th Tank Army), fared no better. Through the combined action of the tactical air force and the naval artillery, the *Panzerdivisionen* were quite simply nailed to the spot. Gunfire from the big 406-mm guns of the battleships *Rodney* and *Nelson* anchored off the Calvados coast was particularly accurate and devastating. The deflagration of a shell of this caliber exploding near a 60-ton tank was so powerful that it was capable of overturning it. Basically, what the Germans had suffered the previous summer at Gela in Sicily or Salerno in Italy was happening all over again in Normandy. In spite of the failure of Epsom, Montgomery had the consolation of knowing that Rommel had risen to the bait. After all, the former victor at El Alamein was holding the main part of the enemy forces around Caen and in the vicinity of Hill 112, the ridge of high ground separating the valley of the Odon from the Orne valley. It only needed the war correspondents to accuse the commander-in-chief of lacking in offensive spirit and to express concern in their articles about the poor territorial gains achieved by the British in their sector. As Bradley wrote, Monty could not justify himself without giving away the secret strategy of his maneuver. The Germans had to be convinced that the Allies' main effort was against Caen.

OPERATION BAGRATION (JUNE-22-AUGUST 19)

While all eyes were fixed on Normandy, another dramatic event was unfolding for the Reich on the eastern front. As he had promised, on June 22, 1944 (the anniversary of Operation Barbarossa), sixteen days after D-Day, Stalin launched Operation Bagration. The aim of this powerful offensive led by the Red Army was to bring about the destruction of several German armies, inflict on the Reich the loss of over half a million men, 1,200 tanks, 8,000 guns and 50,000 vehicles and lead to the capture of around thirty generals. It was Stalingrad all over again!

The battle of the Odon. Here, Scottish soldiers' progress is delayed by the Waffen SS.

The harbors after the storm

(late June 1944)

In spite of the scale of the disaster caused by the strong gale between June 19 and 22, there was no question of losing hope on the Allies' side. It was a far cry from the mood at Dunkirk four years earlier! With the return of fine weather, the Allied command implemented a whole set of measures designed to set things to rights.

Apart from clearing up the beaches, repairing damaged landing craft and restoring the dykes at Omaha and Arromanches by the addition of several extra caissons, it was decided to increase the landings at the small harbors of Lower Normandy (Courseulles, Port-en-Bessin, Grandcamp, Isigny, Saint-Vaast and Barfleur). On June 27, whilst American troops were capturing the port facilities at Cherbourg, ten days behind schedule, Eisenhower took the decision to drop any idea of reconstructing the Omaha mulberry. Meanwhile, the landings continued on the beaches of Saint-Laurent and Colleville, and, with this aim in mind, the gooseberry was strengthened. Any material not yet used for the American artificial harbor was transferred to Arromanches, where assembly was completed by the end of the second week of July. Thanks to all these measures, by the end of June there were 850,000 men, 150,000 vehicles and 600,000 tons of supplies in Normandy. On July 8, six hundred landing craft that had gone aground during the storm were refloated on a big tide, with another hundred two weeks later. On July 26, twenty-three days behind schedule, the first Allied convoy, made up of four liberty-ships, entered the large anchorage in Cherbourg harbor. From that day on, 12,000 tons of stores per day passed through Cherbourg and from mid-September 20,000 tons, after various work had been carried out. Fuel came ashore at the oil terminal at Port-en-Bessin or from England via an underwater pipeline (Pluto) into tanks at the port of Cherbourg.

Big cargo ships that could not be run aground unloaded supplies into amphibious trucks known as DUKWs.

The clean-up of Cherbourg harbor would be followed by the gradual reconstruction of the quays, enabling steam locomotives from the USA, Canada and Great Britain to be unloaded.

In addition to Cherbourg and the artificial harbor at Arromanches, most of the supplies were landed directly on the beaches in LSTs behind the breakwaters. At the end of July, the Americans broke all the records, landing 46,000 men and 8,000 vehicles in a single day on Utah and Omaha beaches alone. The beaches were doing better than Arromanches and Cherbourg put together. By the end of August (D+87), whilst the Allies had reached the Somme, there were some 2,000,000 Allied soldiers, 500,000 vehicles of all kinds and 3,000,000 tons of supplies in France. Of this total, more than half had come directly ashore up the beaches, behind the breakwaters, about 20 per cent through the British artificial harbor, and an equal amount through the small Norman ports (Cherbourg plus the small fishing ports).

LSTs being run aground on the beach at Cherbourg and convoys setting off for the depots.

Canadian soldiers entering Caen, a city destroyed by the aerial bombardment on the evening of July 7.

JULY 1944: THE LIBERATION OF CAEN AND SAINT-LÔ

"If one day Germany is defeated, wrote Goebbels, faced with the Bolshevization of Europe, a horrific Third World War will be inevitable."

Jay W. Baird, *The Mythical World of Nazi War Propaganda*, 1939-1945

The liberation of Caen

(operation Charnwood, July 7-9)

After Operation Epsom, which had finished with no winner or loser, with neither of the belligerents having succeeded in achieving their objective, Montgomery, together with his military staff, devised a plan (Operation Charnwood) to capture the city of Caen.

Allied aircraft above Caen. The bombers had orders to destroy the Panzers.

While the British reassembled their troops for the attack on the important crossroads of Caen, the German police did not remain inactive. As if the fierce fighting that was taking place on the soil of Normandy was a non-event the outcome of which was in no doubt, the *Gestapo* methodically carried on their task of supplying the camps with deportees. With the complicity of the Vichy authorities, the *Besatzungsmacht* (occupying power) continued, as if it would last forever, its conscientious job. According to a report of the International Military Tribunal, on July 2, 1944, whilst in Normandy the Canadians were preparing to conquer Carpiquet, hardly 150 miles away as the crow flies a train filled with 1,800 deportees left Compiègne for the *Reich*. It arrived at Dachau via Bremen and Breslau, 60 hours later, with barely 1,200 survivors. The 600 missing deportees had died of thirst or after scuffles that broke out on the journey. Whereas most of France continued breathing the atmosphere of war until the end of August, by that date Bayeux had been a peaceful oasis again for more than two months.

With scenes of madness on the platforms of Compiègne station as deportees were put onto goods trains, meanwhile in the plain of Caen, General Keller's 3rd Canadian Division Infantry were attempting to take Carpiquet (Operation Windsor) and the western half of the regional capital (Operation Charnwood). On July 6, while the deportees from Compiègne at journey's end were entering organized hell, the British were capturing *die Höhe 112* (coast 112) after an endless battle and the Canadians were taking Carpiquet airfield thirty days behind schedule. To accelerate the capture of Caen by the Anglo-Canadian troops, in the

Position of the *Flak* (german anti-aircraft gun) on the outskirts of Caen. The soldier on the left of the photo calculates the distance to the target using a rangefinder.

evening of July 7,500 bombers dropped more than 7,000 bombs (around 2,500 tons) on the town, already half-destroyed in previous air raids. The next morning another attack took place, this time spearheaded by the naval artillery. This was the coup de grâce which was to wipe the beautiful city of Duke William off the map. Only the Saint-Etienne quarter, where big red crosses were displayed, was relatively spared. It was thus an apocalyptic landscape that the Allied troops discovered on entering the town on July 9.

In spite of the capture of the part of Caen set on the left bank of the Orne, on July 9, after more than a month of fierce fighting, the Allied beachhead still lacked depth. Starting just south of Carteret on the west coast of the Cotentin, the front line ended on the Channel, in the region of Cabourg, passing through Carentan, the north of Saint-Lô, Caumont and Caen. The zone in Allied hands represented no more than a tiny spot on a map of France. In a word, results were rather poor and progress was very slow. The enemy resistance was tougher than expected and each offensive was attempted at high cost. The difficulties of the Allies came not from any lack of courage, which is borne out by the fact that between June 6 and mid-July, Rommel lost more than 100,000 men, an average of 2,500 per day, and 225 tanks! No, the inability to make headway denounced by the journalists was rather due to a combination of factors including, though precisely to what extent it is difficult to say, the bad weather, which prevented the air forces from supporting the ground troops, the hedgerows of the bocage, the technological superiority of the German tanks, the merciless accuracy of the 88-mm guns, and the skill of the Germans in gaining advantage from the terrain.

Following the violent bombing raids of June 6, then those of July 7, many inhabitants of Caen fled the town in flames. Some pushed

Caen destroyed: in the foreground, we can make out the Church of Saint-Jean, and in the background, the Church of Saint-Pierre.

CAEN AFTER THE BOMBARDMENTS

"The city exists. It's a miracle! I recognize, to the west, the Abbaye aux Hommes, on the Normandy front, with the two bell towers intact; to the east is the Abbaye aux Dames, damaged but also still standing. [...] The first inhabitants that we meet watch their liberators – who are also their destroyers – pass by with an expression that is very different from what I saw in Bayeux or Cherbourg. [...] The expression is harrowed, haunted, but relieved. I move forward into the city, into what was the city. Words cannot describe it..."

Jacques Kayser, *A journalist on the Normandy front*

EXCERPT FROM THE MESSAGE OF HOPE BROADCAST TO THE PEOPLE OF CAEN BY THE BRITISH FOREIGN SECRETARY MR. EDEN FOR JULY 14, BASTILLE DAY:

"What until now we have been calling the Resistance is not an isolated movement. It has its roots in the soul of the entire French people. It was at Caen, a few days ago, that we were perhaps best able to realize just how much these sentiments are dear to their hearts.
On the first day of the landing, after four years of German occupation the townspeople of this ancient city of Caen had, we might say, had a foretaste of freedom. Nevertheless they had to put up for a whole month with all the weight of the bombing raids by their own allies. After these trials, when we enter the town, the Frenchmen come to meet us with no recriminations. [...] What we are discovering is the true face of this people. [...] On this day, the last July 14, God willing, when the presence of the enemy keeps us apart, I say: Long live France!"

The life of refugees in the enclosure of the Abbaye aux Hommes.

Fleury quarries, summer 1944.

a wheelbarrow, others towed a handcart, and they sought refuge in the underground galleries at Fleury-sur-Orne. Sited two miles upstream from Caen, these galleries had been carved out of the foot of the escarpment overhanging the valley of the river Orne, during the quarrying of Caen stone. In 1944, most of these dark caves full of oozing damp had been turned into mushroom beds. According to one witness, some 15,000 to 20,000 people went to live in this cold maze. The space was fairly soon occupied in organized fashion and a whole community came to life with its old people's quarter, its large families, its police, its emergency services, its nuns... Each slept either on a mattress or directly on the bed of straw laid out on the ground. A communal kitchen had been set up in a nearby farm. It got its meat supply (up to seven beefs were consumed per day) through groups of volunteers who went out each morning onto the plain to recover and cut up animals killed by shrapnel. During the day, everyone went about their business as usual: collecting wood for the fire, washing clothes and drying them on the bushes, peeling vegetables, commenting on the latest news... The scene made one think of a huge convoy of circus people without the traditional caravans. In this community, whose size varied all the time with the comings and goings, the common behavioral types mixed in all their customary diversity: there were those who started false rumors, those who tried to make themselves useful (helping the sick, the wounded and the old people, and volunteering for odd jobs such as fetching supplies, cleaning and going off in search of medical supplies). The quarries at Fleury were not the only place where there were refugees: others were to be found at the Malherbe grammar school, in underground shelters in cellars, in the Abbey of Saint-Etienne and the farms in the villages on the plain of Caen.

The daily life of the Allied soldiers

In August 1944, the Allied Expeditionary Force confronting the German troops in Normandy comprised some two million soldiers, the majority of which were American. This was over twice the size of the local population.

Among all the Allied armies, the Canadians particularly found favor with the local people. They mostly spoke French and were warmly welcomed without any mistrust by the citizens. A number of lasting links were forged between the liberators and the liberated people.

Despite some reluctance caused by the language barrier and some regrettable incidents, such as the attack on Mers-el-Kébir, the British soon made friends among the local people, even given the bombings and the destruction of the city of Caen. Their army came to the rescue of those who had

Canadian soldier sharing his mess kit with a child.

Normandy: US Air Force doctor examining children.

MESSAGE TO THE FRENCH PEOPLE FROM GENERAL CRERAR, COMMANDER OF THE 1ST CANADIAN ARMY:

"I just want to say to the French people how happy my soldiers of the Canadian army are to be back on French soil. They have come to fight for freedom on your shores. I ask you to welcome them as brothers-in-arms and as friends. You will find among them soldiers of your own blood, the blood of beautiful Normandy where the battle is now raging. They speak your language. You will also find soldiers of Scottish, English, Irish descent. Together, with you, and our British and American allies, we will defeat the Germans."

Eating a hot meal at a table was a luxury.

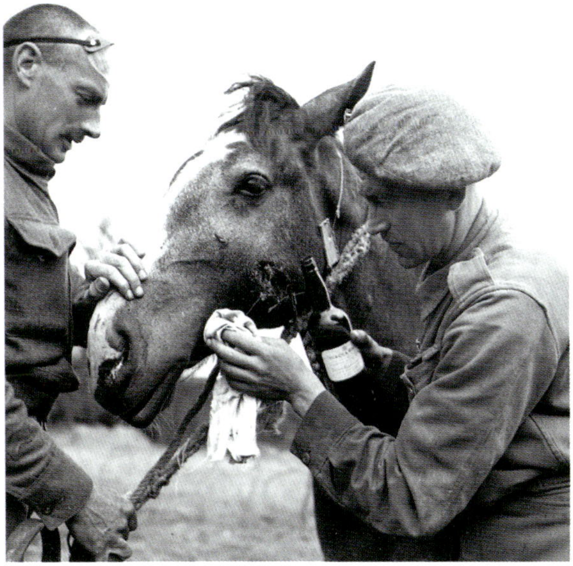

British soldiers: caring for animals.

lost all they owned by creating centers for the distribution of food and blankets. It should be added that the France-England football matches organized, the participation of volunteers in the work of the harvest and the care given to both people and animals by military nurses finally bridged the gap caused by language and prejudice.

Cooking an omelet on a standard portable stove.

As for the Americans, although they were reluctant to drink water from French taps and they searched for numerous ways of fighting against the countless flies from the huge number of empty food cans thrown in the street, they didn't say no to cider or brandy, especially if a young girl was holding the jug... The Americans soon got to know the locals, firstly the children by generously distributing sweets and chewing gum, but also by opening up their medical services to civilians. They were quick to bargain, offering cigarettes or instant coffee for butter, eggs or chickens. They didn't have to wait long for proof of recognition from the people: on Sunday, after Mass, the people of Normandy went to place flowers on the tombs of the soldiers who had come from the distant New World.

The Supreme Commander of Operation Overlord getting washed in the morning in front of reporters.

Finding fresh food was quite an art.

Before embarking on the cross-Channel invasion operation, the chiefs-of-staff of the 1st US Army had accumulated a vast amount of documentation on Normandy. They had also studied in detail the state of public health and the mentality of the Norman people. Here are a few excerpts from the various reports contained in the 1st American Army archives. These documents are interesting because they show how the American military saw the Normandy region and its inhabitants. This text deals with the general hygiene in the region.

Improvised shower.

Collective shower on an American airfield.

"Public health in Normandy leaves something to be desired, although for the time being there is no epidemic in the region. [...] Water should be used with caution: the natives drink and cook with untreated water although, at the same time, they use excrement as fertilizer, which naturally produces pollution of the soil and the water table. In Normandy and more generally in the north-west of France, there are mosquitoes but they do not pass on disease. On the other hand, the flies that exist in large numbers in the pig-sties, byres and milk-parlors do carry enteritis. In the same line of thought, an invasion of lice has to be reported due to reduced resistance among the population, the lack of hygiene (no soap, no hot water, no anti-lice cream). [...] Fleas are also common, as are ticks, moths, cockroaches, rats and wasps in summer. In Normandy, impetigo, scabies, dermatosis and intestinal infections (diarrhea and gastro-enteritis) are especially common owing to the water pollution, the absence of pasteurized milk products and the general lack of hygiene. [...] However, the disease to be feared most is tuberculosis. It is estimated that 1.5 million persons in France currently carry the disease. Then come diphtheria, meningitis and smallpox."

Daily tasks at the front.

Religious service in an American camp.

At the gate of the parish cemetery in Neuilly-la-Forêt (Calvados), two US soldiers from the 29th Division (those who landed on Omaha Beach) talk with the parish priest.

THE MILITARY TRIBUNAL AND AMERICAN SOLDIERS IN NORMANDY

A few days after the invasion, a military tribunal was set up in the American sector. [...] This tribunal was responsible for trying civilian suspects. Between June 12 and August 1, 223 individuals came up for trial. Among them, there were about ten enemy agents, seventy others who were sufficiently dangerous to be handed over to the French authorities for internment. The rest were either small-time collaborationists or German soldiers who had deserted in civilian clothing.

The military tribunal also had the task of trying cases of misconduct among the American soldiers (non-regulation uniforms, infringements of the highway code...). A special section was responsible for more serious offenses (rape, theft, murder, looting, unlawful slaughter of animals...). Between June 12 and August 1, according to 1st US Army reports, the tribunal had to try 117 difficult cases including 22 cases of looting, 17 acts of sexual violence, 25 cases of rape or attempted rape, 10 cases of animal slaughter and as many instances of misuse of fire-arms.

French lesson in a classroom.

Allied airfields in Normandy

Maintaining air superiority over the beachhead was a prerequisite for the success of the Allied operation. The capture of the French airfields (such as Carpiquet, Lessay and Querqueville) as well as the creation of landing strips therefore figured high on the list of objectives for the armies under Eisenhower. Three types of ground installation were planned: emergency landing strips (ELS, 550 yards long), rearming and refueling strips (RRS), and lastly advanced landing grounds (ALG) whose strips were 1100 or 1550 yards long and 36 yards wide. With powerful earth-moving equipment (bulldozers,

Refueling operation at a Normandy airfield.

Cartographic work.

scrapers, mechanical diggers, steamrollers...) at their disposal, the air force sappers could build ALGs (airstrips covered with a square-meshed steel netting, access roads, aircraft parking lots, depots, workshops, barracks for the aircrews) within a week. Covering a surface area of roughly 500 acres, each ALG required for its construction approximately 800 tons of materials (rolls of netting, stakes, clips...), i.e. the equivalent of 400 truckloads!

The engineers of the US Air Force were to build around thirty airfields in Normandy, firstly behind Omaha in Saint-Laurent-sur-Mer (where a fighter-bomber landed on the evening of June 7), then in Saint-Pierre-du-Mont, Cricqueville, Cardonville, Saint-Martin-de-Blangy, Le Molay, Tour-en-Bessin...; behind Utah (including Azeville, Picauville Beuzeville and Brucheville) and in the north of the Cotentin (airfields of the French navy at Querqueville and Maupertus). The final fields built by the Americans in Normandy were those at Gorges, Méautis, Lessay and Saint-Jean-de-Daye, this last one never coming into operation. The first US airfield constructed outside Normandy was opened in Brittany, near Rennes. The British would build strips in Plumetot, Martragny, Bazenville, Le Fresne-Camilly, Amblie, Lantheuil, Villons-les-Buissons, Longues and Saint Aubin d'Arquenay. Opened at the

Bulldozers and scrapers in action: clearing and leveling the ground.

Surfacing the airstrip of an American airfield.

Laying tar paper. Right: The airstrips could not have any defects.

end of June, this last clay strip was used to tow the Horsa gliders recovered in the sector of Ranville, and subsequently re-used in Holland. As for strip B14 at Amblie, it was reserved for the Dakotas for the evacuation of the badly wounded. After Cristot and Ellon, the last of the twenty British airfields in Normandy became operational at Sainte-Honorine-de-Ducy on August 13. The Czech and Polish squadrons fighting in the Royal Air Force were stationed at the Plumetot airfield and the Belgians at Carpiquet, which opened on August 8. The two fighter groups of the Free French Air Force were stationed at Coulombs, the largest British airfield in Normandy.

When the fine weather arrived, enemy number 1 for the pilots was the dust that covered the airfields. Apart from the fact that these dust clouds provided the Germans with excellent indications and choked up the engines to which suitable filters had not be fitted, worst of all they were the cause of numerous collisions on the strips. From mid-July, in order to cure this plague, the strips were given a good watering each night, with water pumped out of the Seulles, the Mue and the Thue.

Laying a metal deck on the viaduct at Cherisy, near Dreux, on the Granville-Paris railway line.

American P-47 fighter-bombers about to take off after refueling and rearming operations.

The liberation of Saint-Lô

(July 18)

During the evening of July 18, after a month at a virtual standstill in the bocage and following interminable, murderous fighting, Bradley's troops seized the important crossroads of Saint-Lô. As with Caen, the town of Saint-Lô was totally destroyed. The capture of the capital of the Manche *département* put an end to the "war of hedgerows", the deadliest ordeal suffered by the 1st US Army during its entire European campaign. By July 20, the Americans had lost 62,000 men including 10,000 killed since the start of the campaign, and the British 35,000 including 6,000 killed.

Saint-Lô: aerial view of the town after the bombardments.

A GI enters Saint-Lô in ruins.

THE JEEP

The jeep, the off-road reconnaissance vehicle of the US Army – solid and responsive with an indestructible engine, practical, easy to maintain and drive, cheap – symbolized the Liberation. It was mass-produced, and 650,000 were made. At the army's request, an amphibious model was produced. It arrived on the Normandy soil transported by gliders early in the morning on June 6 and would prove to be extremely useful, as American reporter Ernie Pyle explains: "Faithful as a dog, solid as a mule, agile as a deer." The German Kübelwagen was a vehicle similar to the jeep.

MAJOR HOWIE

Commander of the 3rd battalion of the 116th infantry regiment of the 29th US division, Major Howie was killed on July 17 as he entered the outskirts of Saint-Lô. The following day, draped in a flag, the body of the Major was transported on a jeep and accompanied the first American soldiers to enter the town. With this gesture, General Gehrard, commander of the 29th division, paid tribute to all the soldiers of his unit who had given their life since the division landed on Omaha beach on the morning of June 6.

A soldier from the 29th division (motto *"Let's go"*) enters Saint-Lô in a vehicle bearing the inscription *"Nihil timemus"*, with the English translation written next to it: *"We fear nothing"*.

Saint-Lô: the station.

THE STENCH OF DEATH

One week after the Battle of Saint-Lô, no one had yet had time to bury the enemy's dead: they could be seen slumped against the steering wheel of the cars in which they had been killed or burned. They were already beginning to decompose and the air was filled with the heavy, sickly stench of death. We couldn't escape the smell and it seemed to invade our quarters.

Above: GIs during the Battle of the Hedgerows, July 1944.
Below: Lt. General Manton S. Eddy, Commanding Officer of the 9th US Infantry Division, in a jeep, Les Champs-de-Losque, July 26,1944.

Opposite: A wounded GI having his foot dressed in the Normandy bocage.

Operation Goodwood

(July 18-21)

In the second half of July, thanks to the reinforcements that had arrived in the meantime on the beaches or through the artificial harbor, the Allied commanders once again prepared to break out in the sectors of Caen and Saint-Lô. This was the very moment, when the Allies were preparing to regain the operational initiative, that Rommel chose to disappear altogether from Normandy after his car was machine-gunned by a British plane. Three days later, it was Hitler's turn to be the victim of an attempt on his life, in eastern Prussia. This event would not, in fact, make much difference to the situation on the western front. It was in this context that, on July 18, the British units launched their second outflanking operation around Caen, this time on the eastern flank (Operation Goodwood). Reserves mustered in the half-circle going from the river Dives and comprising the eastern end of the beachhead were gigantic. With three armored divisions, 700 guns and 2,000 bombers overhead, Goodwood remains the most massive operation of the entire Normandy campaign.

Operation Goodwood: flail tank (mine-clearing tank).

Operation Goodwood was the largest battle led by the Allies in Normandy. Here, a bomber flies over the Colombelles steelworks.

Marshal Rommel, commander-in-chief of Army Group B, was wounded in a car accident on July 17. "Am 17.7 verunglückte der OB der H. Gr. B, Gen. Feldm. Rommel durch einen Autofall."

Official *Wehrmacht* communiqué on German radio

The Allied air forces were the Germans' nightmare in Normandy.

The counter-attack of the defenders at the launch of Operation Goodwood was fierce.

The day after the July 20 attack against the Führer, this is what Goebbels wrote:
"The Führer has left his shelter to come and meet me; I'm moved... One can but feel extreme affection for him. He is the greatest historical genius alive in our time."

***Diaries*, 23 July 1944**

After *der Fall von Caen* (the fall of Caen), on July 18, in spite of the scale of resources deployed, the southward thrust at the German positions (Falaise) was soon held up on the outskirts of the capital of Lower Normandy. The bad weather transformed the Normandy campaign into a quagmire, and the solid, deep German defense organized on several lines, together with the scale of the losses (over 5,000 men and 400 tanks), forced Monty to put an end to the operation. The results were far poorer than had been predicted. Even though the limits of the British beachhead had been pushed back by six miles towards the south and the city of Caen had been completely liberated, the large Caen-Falaise plain, which would have been so useful to the airmen, remained in the hands of the Germans. Nevertheless, Goodwood was not a failure in strategic terms: like the previous offensives, it was part of a long-term plan to try to wear out the enemy forces before the final confrontation.

SS prisoner after being searched.
Below: **Goodwood cost the British over 400 tanks.**

The closing of the beaches and harbors

(November 1944)

With the onset of winter, it became impossible to continue bringing supplies ashore on the beaches. The Allied command therefore took the decision to close the Normandy beaches in mid-November 1944. One month previously, following an increase in the traffic from Cherbourg and the capture of further installations (Granville, Morlaix, Le Havre, Dieppe), the Admiralty had stopped using the small ports in Lower Normandy, and these were handed back to the French authorities on November 9, 1944. In turn, the Arromanches mulberry was closed on November 19 and, from early December, work began to dismantle the platforms on piles and the floating piers. At the same time, several Phoenix caissons from the Arromanches artificial harbor were towed to Walcheren island to breach gaps created in the polder dykes by overhead bombing. Since the end of the war, doubts have been raised, especially by the Americans, as to the utility of the artificial harbors. The US command, deprived of its mulberry because of the storm, demonstrated in the Channel, as it had already done in Sicily and in Italy, that it was possible to unload vast quantities of equipment in the shelter of a solid breakwater by directly running LSTs and a flotilla of DUKWs (amphibious trucks) aground. Despite this criticism, artificial harbors remain one of the most significant innovations of the Second World War. With the mulberries, the Allies had a unique tool that enabled them to create a real strategic element of surprise, a decisive factor in the success of any military undertaking. By landing on a free coast, where the Germans were not expecting them, the Allies brought about the failure of the entire costly defensive system of the adversary which was mainly focused on the major port installations, the natural entrance to the continent when arriving by sea.

American poster inviting the people to buy bonds in order to bring an end to the war.

It is difficult to say today whether it was the British or the Americans who performed the greatest feat during the summer of 1944. The British designed, built, towed and assembled Arromanches harbor, the cornerstone of Operation Overlord, whilst the Americans managed to land many more vehicles, ammunition and soldiers directly onto the beaches behind simple breakwaters than had arrived via the mulberries.

Providing the armies with fuel supplies

(Pluto)

The question of fuel supplies, a vital one for any modern army, took first place in the Overlord plan along with the capture of airfields and continental ports. It must be said that the fuel requirements (petrol for the vehicles, kerosene for the air force, diesel fuel for the ships' engines) were colossal, estimated at 15,000 tons per day on D+41 (July 15). To avoid any shortage for the 200,000 vehicles that would be present by that time on the beachhead, and to have advance supplies equivalent to two

Cherbourg. Oil terminal: unloading a tanker that has come directly from the United States.

Cherbourg. Oil terminal. Each pipeline transported a specific type of fuel.

Cherbourg. Wiew of the large sea wall along which the tankers docked to unload their various shipments, as illustrated by the bundle of pipelines running along the top of the seawall.

weeks' average consumption, it was necessary to unload more than 500,000 tons of petroleum products on the Normandy coast between June 6 and July 15 in the face of enemy counter-attacks.

In order to pull off this tour de force, the chiefs-of-staff decided upon several supply systems. During the first ten days following the assault, with no installations as yet available, fuel was unloaded directly onto the beaches in metal jerrycans from LCTs that ran aground. Meanwhile, the navy set up an anchorage for petrol-tankers off Sainte-Honorine-des-Pertes connected by two sea lines (flexible piping laid on the sea bed) to tanks sited on the rising ground of the Mont Cauvin, a few miles to the rear. Nearby at Port-en-Bessin an oil terminal was set up along the piers also to feed the Mont Cauvin oil-tanks through rigid pipes. Known as the minor system, this initial installation was shared by the Americans and the British.

This initial means of supply was scheduled to be phased out on July 15 and replaced by what was known as the major system installations in the port of Cherbourg. With a higher flow rate, the major system would be simultaneously fed by large oil-tankers anchoring at the Querqueville pier terminal, used by the French navy before the war, and by an undersea pipeline known as Pluto. Owing to the scale of the destruction of the port installations, the first tanker did not come alongside the pier until July 25, a month after the capture of the port. As for Pluto, its installation across the Channel between the Isle of Wight and Cherbourg, a distance of approximately 60 miles, was behind schedule from the outset. This operation of unwinding ten flexible pipelines along the seabed had never actually been attempted before. In theory, each tube was to transfer 300 tons a day, and according to the initial plan, the first pipe should have reached Cherbourg by D+12 (18 June). The belated capture of the fortress, bad weather and the slowness of the clearing-up operations in the Cherbourg area meant that Pluto was only pressurized at the beginning of August, six weeks late. This delay meant that there was a shortfall of over 100,000 tons of fuel, which did not however cause too many problems since the Americans' progress in the bocage was slow and hence their fuel consumption was lower than expected. The late implementation and under-performance of the major system due to problems with Pluto obliged the high command to increase unloading operations

Resupplying a depot from a fuel tanker. Jerrycans were redistributed by tankers to the front and the airfields.

at the Port-en-Bessin terminal, in the small harbors (Courseulles) and especially on Utah and Omaha beaches. With the movement of the front it became necessary to extend the network of pipelines from the storage pool at Cherbourg, initially southwards in the direction of Avranches and the Loire. Then in early August, General Bradley changed the initial path and moved Pluto towards Paris and the Seine. Nearly 7,500 sappers of the American army with the help of 1,500 German prisoners-of-war were requisitioned to complete the earth-removing and welding work. After the capture of the port installations at Le Havre, Dieppe, Boulogne and Antwerp and the laying of a second undersea pipeline between Dungeness and Boulogne, the Allies were able to put their minds at rest.

Welding pipes.

Caring for the wounded

THE HOSPITAL CAMP IN LA CAMBE

"The US military hospital camp in La Cambe was set up along the road leading to Cherbourg. It opened on June 15 and, once completed, comprised 400 beds under tents, around forty doctors and the same number of nurses. Around a hundred operations on average were performed every day on six operating tables."

Lee Miller

Transporting the wounded by ambulance.
Below: Surgical operation in a tent.

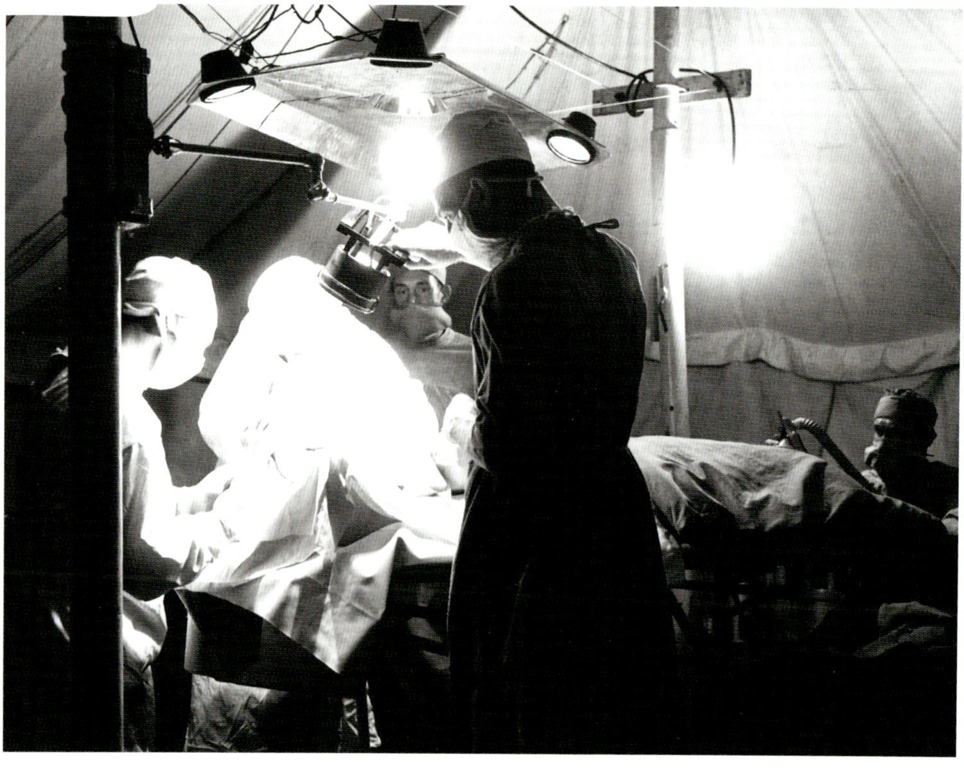

US military hospital camp in Normandy.

Left: Evacuating the wounded by boat to England.
Right: The most seriously wounded were transported by Dakota air ambulance.

Reporting and photographing the war

"Complete wartime co-ordination and perfect co-operation can never be achieved between the press and military authorities. For the commander secrecy is a defensive weapon; to the press it is anathema. The task is to develop a procedure that takes into account an understanding of both viewpoints. [...] In the handling of the press, the American practice was to provide every facility that would permit an individual to go wherever he wanted, wherever he wanted. Everyone knew that we weren't trying to cover up mistakes or stupidity."

D. D. Eisenhower, *Crusade in Europe*

Soldier from the 1st Polish armored division filming the departure of his unit for Falaise.

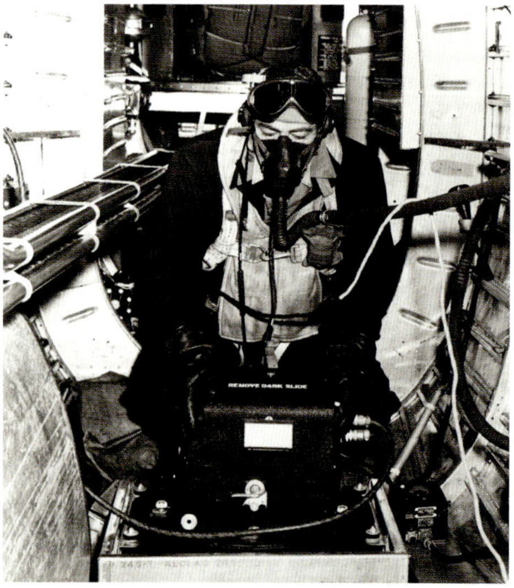

US cameraman on the cover plate of the base for German torpedo boats (Cherbourg arsenal).
Right: Aerial view taken at high altitude. These were often used to check the effectiveness of an aerial bombardment.

US cameraman accompanying a section given the task of cleaning the buildings of a farm in the Cotentin.

Poster: *"Good news from home, more production."*

AUGUST 1944: BREAK-OUT AND VICTORY

"The state of the front is worse than regrettable.
In the west, the situation has become critical."

Goebbels, *Diaries*, 3 August 1944

In early 1944, there were 1.6 million Allied soldiers in Normandy, including 900,000 Americans with 176,000 vehicles and 660,000 British with 156,000 vehicles. On the enemy side, taking into account the reinforcements that had arrived since June 6 (around thirty divisions that had joined the six already in Normandy), von Kluge (Rommel's successor) had around the same number of large units, but the German formations were scanty in comparison with those of the Allies.

General Patton, commander of the 3rd US Army, a formation given the task of exploiting the collapse of the front (Operation Cobra) achieved by Bradley's 1st Army. The most notable figure of the Allied camp, Patton commanded the American assault troops in North Africa and the 7th Army during the invasion of Sicily. For tacticians today, Patton remains the embodiment of boldness, impetuosity and surprise.

Operation Cobra

(July 25-30)

If Goodwood was a disappointing operation, on the other hand Cobra, code name of the break-out undertaken by the Americans in the sector of Saint-Lô from July 25, was a stupendous success. Preceded, as was Goodwood, by an exceptionally powerful preparatory air strike, Cobra opened the breach and led the Americans into Coutances on July 28, then Granville and Avranches on July 31. Finally, after 55 days of fighting, the moment so long awaited by Eisenhower and the whole world had come: the western flank of the German defenses collapsed. This collapse surpassed even the most optimistic predictions. Ignoring the suffering of the men and the losses which, since June 6, had risen to almost 130,000 soldiers, Hitler ordered von Kluge to make the most of the over-deployment of the US forces and advance towards Avranches to cut off the units of the 3rd US Army (that of Patton) that had unwisely ventured into Brittany.

Line of trucks used to bring supplies to the 3rd US Army.

Trucks transporting the supplies of the 3rd US Army from the beaches and from Cherbourg harbor.

Marauder, a twin-engine medium bomber. As with Goodwood, the resources implemented during Cobra were vast (aircraft, armored vehicles, artillery and infantry).

OPERATION SPRING

To support the launch of Cobra, Eisenhower asked Monty to launch a new offensive, after the disappointment of Goodwood. Led by the Ist Canadian Army and known as Spring, this operation, which began on July 25 south of Caen, aimed to capture the town of Falaise, still 12 miles away. The attack had barely been launched when the Canadians came up against an impenetrable, savage and deadly defense which caused them to lose 1,500 men on July 25 alone. This forced Monty to put an end to the operation on the very evening that it had started. After the raid on Dieppe, Spring would remain the most costly attack launched by the Canadian army.

Avranches and the Mortain counter-attack

At the beginning of August, the American forces, deployed over more than 80 miles between Cherbourg and Pontaubault at the gateway to Brittany, constituted a relatively thin flank on a level with Avranches. This vulnerable sector did not go unnoticed by Hitler, who ordered General von Kluge to launch a mainly tank counter-offensive westwards from the region of Mortain, i.e. in the direction of the Bay of the Mont Saint Michel. The aim of the operation was to cut the US forces in two and to isolate in the

The *Wehrmacht*'s final days in Normandy.

Liberation of Avranches by Patton's army (late July).

Brittany peninsula the units that had been unwisely committed there. It was indeed a unique opportunity and an extremely tempting gamble.

Forewarned of enemy intentions by his wire-tapping department who had decoded the wireless messages, Bradley was on his guard and had guns at the ready. Launched in the fog in the early hours of August 7, with the help of half a dozen armored divisions, or roughly 400 *Panzers*, *Lüttich*, code name of the large-scale operation organized down to the smallest details by Hitler, was blocked the very same day. Equipped with anti-tank rockets placed under the wings, the *Jabos* (as the German soldiers called the Allied fighter-bombers), had worked wonders. Once again, the enemy had wasted about fifty tanks in a risky not to say desperate operation due to the lack of adequate air cover.

As von Kluge wrote to Hitler a few hours before committing suicide, the *Angriff* [the attack] in the direction of Avranches against the 1st US Army had been impossible to execute and had not the slightest chance of succeeding. Doomed almost from

German prisoners packed into a church in the south of the Manche *département*.
Opposite: Offensive (Operation Bluecoat) led by the British troops in the bocage (here the sector of Mount Pinçon) which aimed to provide support on their left for the American units advancing towards Avranches across the Cotentin.

the outset, Operation *Lüttich* was to be the Germans' final effort in Normandy before they withdrew.

Meanwhile, on the other flank, Montgomery launched Operation Totalize in the Caen sector on the evening of August 7. Assigned to the 1st Canadian Army, the aim of this offensive was to break out southwards through the enemy lines. As it turned out, after several days of fierce fighting, the impetus of the Canadians, with temporary support from a Polish armored division, was broken and the undertaking tailed off about fifteen miles outside Falaise. Without wasting any time, a second tank offensive was launched. Code-named Tractable, this new thrust had the same objective as before: to break through the German positions blocking the route to Falaise. Four days after Tractable was launched, that is on August 18, the Anglo-Canadian troops finally prized open the gates to the town.

The Falaise pocket

While these military events were taking place, the American armed forces were pursuing their victorious advance in Brittany whilst another section headed off towards the Loire. After liberating Rennes and Le Mans, the US units headed off straight towards the Seine and Paris, joined by the 2nd French Armored Division under General Leclerc, who had landed early in August at Utah Beach. There was no more time to be lost. When Montgomery, after two months of vain attempts, finally broke through the enemy's defensive positions south of Caen and

Prayer and asking for protection from the Almighty.

Opposite: Column of Allied armored vehicles heading for the village of Pierrefitte-en-Cinglais (7 miles west of Falaise) with a fighter-bomber flying overhead.

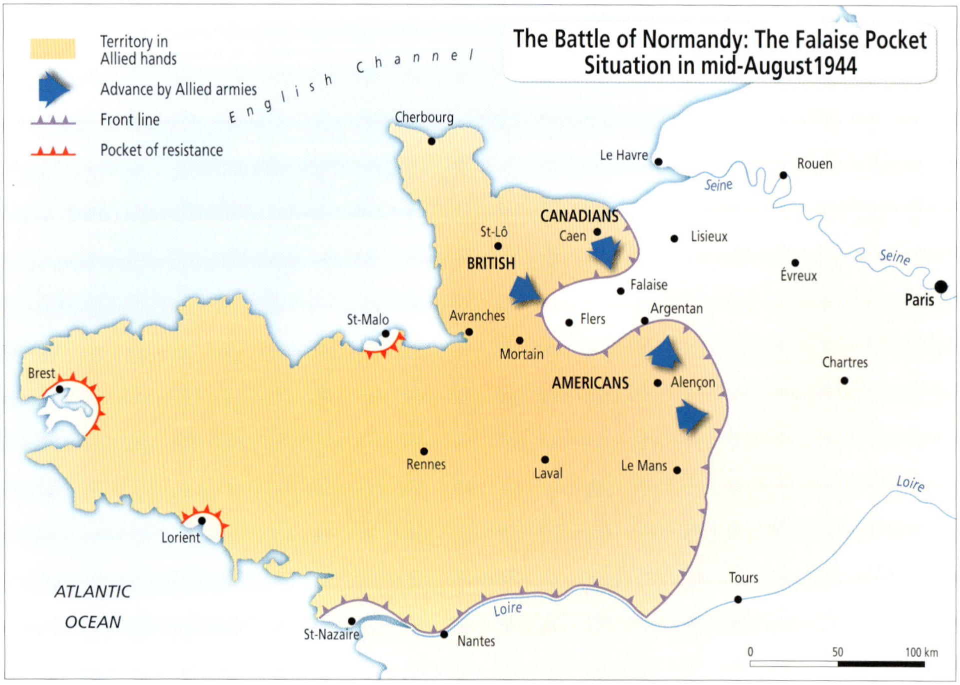

American convoys making their way up to Chambois.

"Rommel's army was routed. [...] The combats between the British and the Germans were intense and savage in the extreme. It was a battle to the death."

Churchill, *Memoirs*

started bringing heavy pressure to bear in the direction of Falaise, the Americans prepared to attack the German armies from behind. The two jaws of the pincer drew inexorably closer. However, in spite of the Allied efforts, the Falaise Gap, sealed at Chambois in the evening of August 19 after the Canadians and the Americans had met, was not carried out as promptly as it should have been. A sizable

Saint-Lambert after the fighting.

portion, maybe as much as half of the German forces, had made their escape and crossed the Seine, in spite of the destruction of the bridges. The battle for Normandy was definitively over two days later, on August 21 in a farmyard at Tournai-sur-Dives, when fifty thousand men, comprising all that remained of the two big German formations that had fought against the Allies in Normandy during the summer of 1944, were captured in the pocket.

STALINGRAD AND FALAISE

Despite the disaster suffered by the Wehrmacht, the consequences of this defeat were not as great as they might have been for the Allies:
"In Stalingrad, an entire army was destroyed, its leader and some 25 generals surrendered. In Normandy, there was no mass surrender. Most of the generals and the staff of the 7th Army escaped. Nor was there a similar capitulation, because there was no question of Hausser's army laying down its weapons."

Chester Wilmot, *The Struggle for Europe*

Prisoners of war

On D-Day, POW camps were set up on the edge of the beaches. Later a large camp for 10,000 prisoners was opened in the American sector, at Foucarville, followed by another, a few days later, at Valognes. At the end of June, a third big camp was set up at Formigny (to the rear of Omaha Beach), then, as the advance progressed, two new camps were opened, one at Saint-Jean-de-Daye and the other at Saint-Jores (at the end of July).

By mid-June, in the 1st Army sector, the Americans had taken a little over 3,000 prisoners. Two weeks later, after Cherbourg

German prisoners in a transit camp.

On the way to England or America.

had fallen, the number was in excess of 40,000, and it passed the 60,000 mark by the end of July, at the time of the break-out at Avranches. Out of this total, 55,000 POWs were sent to Britain on board LSTs (the remaining 5,000 were the badly wounded). Apart from digging graves, the prisoners of war were employed on a rota basis by the health service of the American armies (setting up field hospitals).

German prisoners waiting to set off, near Cherbourg.

The routed Wehrmacht

Pursuing their onward march with the 2nd French Armored in the lead, the Allies entered Paris on August 24. With the arrival of the American soldiers on the banks of the Loire (in the first week of August) on one side and the crossing of the Seine by Patton's troops (during the night of August 19-20) on the other, the Overlord plan launched on June 6 was fully achieved. At the end of August (D+87), Eisenhower could once again rub his hands: he had accomplished the first part of his mission in north-western Europe three days ahead of the schedule devised in London in the spring of 1944. Another campaign was beginning, the campaign for the liberation of France, with Dragoon, the landing on the shores of Provence carried out by Franco-American forces on August 15, 1944, marking its first stage.

Retreat of the *Wehrmacht*.

Allied propaganda photo which aimed to show that even the supermen in the *Panzer Hitlerjugend* (Hitler Youth) division did not hesitate to surrender.

THE GRAND ALLIANCE

"The Anglo-American alliance of the Second World War is probably the most successful in all history. [...] The association's aim was to defeat the Axis powers. The agreements secured on the way in which the war should be carried out were no more than compromises, and it is neither surprising nor disturbing that the British and American operations did not always coincide. What is striking is the fact that their leaders managed to take joint decisions and that they applied them in all loyalty."

M. Blumenson, *The Battle of the Generals*

The cost of the victory in Normandy

The big showdown in Normandy was a murderous one for both sides, and the statistics are comparable with those of the First World War: it was the same blood-bath. By August 31, the Allied losses (killed, missing or prisoners and wounded) totaled 225,000, with 73,000 killed (33,000 British, including Canadians and Polish, and 40,000 Americans) and 153,000 wounded (58,000 British and 95,000 Americans).

In the other camp, according to what General Montgomery wrote in his book

Despite 20,000 civilian victims and unquestionable violence during the fighting, the people of Normandy remained grateful to the allied soldiers who had come to liberate them. A couple of Normans pay their respect in front of the remains of an American soldier who fell on the side of the road going from Carentan to Saint-Hilaire-Petitville.

Nuremberg (April 1945), one of the centers of Nazism, where Nazi Party congresses were regularly held, accompanied by solemn parades with flags, light shows, military music and frenzied crowds. The road which led the democracies to victory was long and was traveled at great human cost.

Normandy to Baltic, the *Wehrmacht* lost around 400,000 men, half of them prisoners. The number of losses of vehicles of all kinds amounted to 22,000, including 1,500 *Panzers* and 2,000 pieces of artillery (cannons, *Flaks* and anti-tank weapons).

Although a decisive event in the Second World War, the battle of Normandy did not bring an end to the conflict. Another 8 months of hard fighting was to follow after *der Kessel von Falaise* [the Falaise Gap] before the 3rd *Reich* would capitulate unconditionally. However, as Colonel Stacey, the Canadian army's official historian, points out, in Normandy a death blow was administered to the morale of the German army. This time there was no doubt about it: Falaise was indeed the beginning of the end.

After costly sacrifices, the Allied coalition emerged victorious, and the leader of this coalition was America. By revealing the United States' military supremacy, Normandy heralded the post-war world. For the United States as well as for Europe, a new day dawned on the shores of the Channel during the summer of 1944.

BIBLIOGRAPHY

INVASIONS BEFORE OVERLORD

Jay W. Baird, *The Mythical World of Nazi War Propaganda, 1939-1945*, Minneapolis, University of Minnesota Press, 1974.
Joseph Goebbels, *Reden*, Düsseldorf, Helmut Heiber, 2 Bänder, 1972.
Joseph Goebbels, *The Goebbels Diaries*, London, Hamish Hamilton, 1948.
Hans A. Jacobsen, "Les Buts et la politique de guerre de Hitler", from *Revue d'histoire de la Deuxième Guerre mondiale*, No. 63.
Manfred Messerschmidt, "La Stratégie allemande (1939-1945)", from *Revue d'histoire de la Deuxième Guerre mondiale*, No. 100, 1975.
Samuel E. Morison, *Operations in North African Waters. History of United States Naval Operations in World War II*, vol. II, Boston, Little Brown and Co, 1981.
Samuel E. Morison, *Sicily, Salerno, Anzio. History of United States Naval Operations in World War II*, vol. IX, Boston, Little Brown and Co, 1981.
Ernie Pyle, *Brave Men*, New York, Henry Holt, 1975.
Jacques Robchon, *Le Corps expéditionnaire français en Italie, 1943-1944*, Paris, Presses de la Cité, 1981.
Percy Ernst Schramm, *Kriegstagebuch des Oberkommandos der Wehrmacht (1940-1945)* [War Diary of the High Command of the *Wehrmacht*], Teilband 1: 1944-1945, München, 1982, vol. IV/7.
Colonel C. P. Stacey, *La Campagne de la victoire. Les opérations dans le nord-ouest de l'Europe (1944-1945)*, vol. III, Ottawa, Imprimerie de la Reine, 1966.
Die Wehrmachtberichte 1939-1945, Band 3, 1. Januar bis 9. Mai 1945, Köln, 1989.

THE ATLANTIC WALL

Heinrich Breloer, *Speer et Hitler. L'architecte du diable*, Paris, Albin Michel, 2006.
Rémy Desquesnes, *Atlantikwall et Südwall: la défense allemande sur le littoral français (1941-1944)*, 2 volumes, Université de Caen, 1987.
Rémy Desquesnes, *Le Mur de l'Atlantique: du Mont-Saint-Michel au Tréport*, Rennes, Edilarge, 2004.
Rémy Desquesnes, *Histoire secrète du Mur de l'Atlantique*, Fécamp, Editions des Falaises, 2003.
Xaver Dorsch, *Organisation Todt in Frankreich*, MS-B-670, Freiburg-im-Breisgau.
Joseph Goebbels, *Journal 1943-1945*, Paris, Tallandier, 2005.
Colin Partridge, *Hitler's Atlantik Wall*, Guernesey, D. I. Publications, 1976.
Generalleutnant Rudolf Schmetzer, *Bericht über den Ausbau des Atlantik-Walles*, MS-B-668 and 669.
Albert Speer, *Au cœur du IIIe Reich*, Paris, Fayard, 1971.
Alan Wilt, *The Atlantic Wall: German Defenses in the West, 1941-1944*, University of Michigan, 1969.

OPERATION OVERLORD

German archives: Mémorial de Caen.
Joseph Balkovski, *Omaha Beach D-Day, June 6, 1944*, Stackpole Books, 2004.
E. Belfield et H. Essame, *Normandie été 1944*, Paris, Presses de la Cité, 1966.
Yves Blanchard, *Le Radar 1904-2004*, Paris, Ellipses, 2004.
Anthony Cave Brown, *Bodyguard of Lies*, London, W. H. Allen, 1976.
David D. Eisenhower, *Croisade en Europe*, Paris, Robert Laffont, 1957.
Major Friedrich Hayn, *Die Invasion: von Cotentin bis Falaise*, Heidelberg, 1954.
Erwin Rommel, *La Guerre sans haine*. Volume II: *Les Années de la défaite*, Châtillon-sous-Bagneux, Le Livre contemporain, Imprimerie S.E.G., 1960.
Général Walter Warlimont, *Cinq ans au G.Q.G. de Hitler*, Paris, Elsevier, 1975.
A Study in command, FMS-B308, Washington D.C.

THE BATTLE OF NORMANDY

P. Bauduin, "Vingt aérodromes pour la victoire", from *Icare*, No. 113.
Eddy Bauer, *Histoire controversée de la Seconde Guerre mondiale*, 10 vol., Paris, Atlas, 1980.
Martin Blumenson, *Breakout and Pursuit*, Washington D.C., 1961.

Martin Blumenson, *La Bataille des généraux*, Condé-sur-Noireau, Corlet, 1983.
Omar M. Bradley, *A General's Life*, New York, Simon and Schuster, 1983.
William B. Breuer, *Hitler's Fortress Cherbourg*, New York, Stein and Day, 1984.
Commandant K. Edwards, *Opération Neptune*, Paris, La Jeune Parque, 1947.
David D. Eisenhower, *Les Opérations en Europe du Corps expéditionnaire allié*, Paris, Berger-Levrault, 1947.
Major L. F. Ellis, *Victory in the West*. Vol. 1: *The Battle of Normandy*, London, Her Majesty's Stationery Office, 1962.
Carlo d'Este, *Decision in Normandy*, New York, Darnes and Noble, 1963.
Carlo d'Este, *Eisenhower, a Soldier's Life*, New York, Henry Holt, 2002.
Jean Galtier-Boissière, *Mon Journal pendant l'Occupation*, Paris, La Jeune Parque, 1944.
Joseph Goebbels, *Journal 1945*, Paris, Tallandier, 2005.
Gordon A. Harrison, *Cross Channel Attack*, Washington D.C., Office of the Chief of Military Office, 1951.
Hervie Haufler, *Codebreakers' Victory*, New York, New American Library, 2003.
Philip Henshall, *Hitler's Rocket Sites*, London, Robert Hale, 1985.
Ralph Ingersoll, *Ultra secret*, Paris, La Jeune Parque, 1947.
Jacques Kayser, *Un journaliste sur le front de Normandie. Carnet de route, juillet-août 1944*, Paris, Arléa, 1991.
Basil H. Liddell Hart, *Histoire de la Seconde Guerre mondiale*, Paris, Fayard, 1973.
Gerald Linderman, *The World within War. America's Combat Experience in World War II*, Cambridge, Massachusetts, Harvard University Press, 1999.
John C. McManus, *The Americans at Normandy*, New York, Tom Doherty Associates Book, 2004.
Montgomery, *Mémoires du Maréchal Montgomery*, Paris, Plon, 1958.
Williamson Murray, Allan Millett, *A War to be Won*, Cambridge, Harvard University Press 2000.
Richard Overy, *Why the Allies Won?* New York, Norton, 1995.
R. Ruppenthal, *Logistical Support of the Armies*. Vol. II, Washington D.C., OCMH, 1959.
Milton Schulman, *La Défaite allemande à l'ouest*, Paris, Payot, 1948.
Gerhard L. Weinberg, *Visions of Victory. The hopes of eight World War II Leaders*, Cambridge University Press, 2005.
Chester Wilmot, *La Lutte pour l'Europe*, Paris, Fayard, 1953.
Royal Air Force, *Narrative*. Vol. III: *The Landings in Normandy*, Air Historical Branch.

PHOTOGRAPHIC CREDITS

Akg images: pages 85, 103 (b), 151 • **Akg-images / / TT News Agency / SVT:** page 93 (b) • **Archives municipales de Caen:** 156, 176 (b) • **Bibliothèque nationale de France/Cabinet des Estampes:** 11 (b), 47, 66, 67, 103 (t), 108 (b), 118, 124, 192 • **Bundesarchiv:** 16 (b), 40, 44, 49, 51, 52, 57 (t), 63, 64, 76, 85, 115, 157, 180, 181, 208, 214 (2e), back cov. (bl) • **D.R.:** 54 (t), 59 (tl), 126 • **ECPAD:** 33, 38 (b) • **Imperial War Museum:** 13, 15, 16 (t), 19, 23 (t), 42, 59 (tr), 61, 65, 71, 81, 82, 83, 94, 95, 96, 97, 98, 105 (b), 106, 110-111, 116, 117, 122, 127, 128 (t), 133 (b), 140, 149, 150, 156, 159, 163, 164 (b), 165 (tl; br), 167, 169 (t), 179, 182 (t), 201, 215 (t), back cov. (bc) • **Keele University:** 75, 122, 135 • **Koninklijke Bibliothek, den Haag:** 45 • **Le Mémorial de Caen:** 7, 20, 32 (b), 48, 56 (t), 87, 88, 89, 90, 104 (b), 128 (b), 183, 192, 206, 214 (b) • **Le Mémorial de Caen/Fonds russe:** 23 (b), 29 • **Le Mémorial de Caen/Signal:** 12 (h) • NARA: cov. (b), 4, 17, 18, 24 (t), 25, 32 (t), 35 (b), 55, 56 (b), 57 (b), 58, 60, 68, 70, 72, 73, 84, 86, 92, 99, 100-101, 102, 104, 113, 114, 119 (b), 120, 125, 129, 130, 131, 132, 133 (t), 134, 136, 137, 138, 139 (b), 141, 142, 143, 144, 145, 146, 147, 148, 152, 153, 162, 164 (t), 165 (tr), 167, 168, 169 (b), 170, 171, 172, 173, 174, 175, 184, 185, 186, 187, 188, 189, 190 (b), 191, 192, 195, 196, 197, 199, 200, 202, 204, 207, 210, 211, 214 (3e), 215 (b), back cov. (t et br) • **Public Archives of Canada:** cov. (t), 8, 10, 11 (t), 12 (b), 27, 28, 30, 31, 34, 35 (t), 37, 38 (t), 39, 53, 107, 109, 119 (t), 139 (t), 154, 158, 161, 178, 190 (t), 203, 205, 209, 214 (t), 215 (c) • **Roger-Viollet:** 54 (b) • **USAF:** 21, 24 (b), 35 (b), 74, 78, 79, 80, 105 (t), 112, 165 (tr), 169 (b; c), 170, 190 (br).

Colorized photos (Éditions Ouest-France/Graph&ti): cov. (b) and back cover, pages 4, 92, 100-101, 110-111, 119, 148, 173, 176, 177, 181.

ACKNOWLEDGMENTS

Archives de guerre, D. Forget - Philippe Trombetta - Marie-Claude Berthelot - Jacques Soussy - Philippe Patrice

Contents

Éditeur : Matthieu Biberon
Coordination éditoriale : Caroline Brou
Collaboration éditoriale : Jeanne Durand
Conception graphique et mise en page :
Elise Druon-Petitbon - EliLoCom
Cartographie : Patrick Mérienne
Photogravure : Graph&ti, Rennes (35)
Impression : SEPEC, Péronnas (01) - 08311240201

ISBN 978-2-7373-9022-7 - N° d'éditeur : 11117.01.01.03.24
Dépôt légal : mars 2024
Imprimé en France
Retrouvez-nous sur editions.ouest-france.fr

PEFC
10-31-1470
Certifié PEFC
Ce produit est issu de forêts gérées durablement et de sources contrôlées
www.pefc-france.org